James Mills Peirce

The Elements of Logarithms

With an Explanation of the three and four Place Tables of logarithmic and trigonometric Functions

James Mills Peirce

The Elements of Logarithms
With an Explanation of the three and four Place Tables of logarithmic and trigonometric Functions

ISBN/EAN: 9783337131142

Printed in Europe, USA, Canada, Australia, Japan

Cover: Foto ©ninafisch / pixelio.de

More available books at **www.hansebooks.com**

THE ELEMENTS

OF

LOGARITHMS

WITH AN EXPLANATION OF THE

THREE AND FOUR PLACE TABLES

OF LOGARITHMIC AND TRIGONOMETRIC
FUNCTIONS

BY

JAMES MILLS PEIRCE

UNIVERSITY PROFESSOR OF MATHEMATICS IN HARVARD UNIVERSITY

BOSTON
PUBLISHED BY GINN BROTHERS
1874

Entered according to Act of Congress, in the year 1873, by

JAMES MILLS PEIRCE,

In the Office of the Librarian of Congress, at Washington.

PREFACE.

THIS little book is meant chiefly for beginners; but I have also had in view the wants of more advanced students who are seeking to refresh and deepen their knowledge. The sections included in brackets are inserted for their benefit; and it is my purpose to add, in a future edition, chapters on the natural system, series, and the errors incident to simple interpolation, so as to make the book a complete manual of all that can be considered as belonging to the elements of the subject.

Logarithms ought not to be comprised, as they often are, in the midst of a treatise on algebra. For, in the first place, they are not algebraic functions; and, besides this, the student is unlikely to form an adequate comprehension of their purpose or to appreciate the importance of acquiring skill in the use of his tables, if he takes them up in the course of a study to which they have no application. If logarithms must needs be combined with any other branch of mathematics, their true alliance, on grounds both theoretical and practical, is not with algebra, but with trigonometry. But it seems to me desirable that so important a subject should be studied by itself, and studied fully and thoroughly; and the aim of the teacher should be the double one of expounding the doctrine of logarithms in a concise, accurate, and clear form, and of inculcating and enforcing good practical principles in the use of tables. It has been my endeavor, accordingly, in writing these pages, not, of course, to convert the learner into an accomplished computer, but to set him on the right road towards becoming such if he pleases, and, at all events, to lead him to form the sound habits of work without which little beneficial discipline is derivable from this study.

I hope that teachers who are preparing pupils for Harvard College, where logarithms are now required for admission, will find that this volume furnishes them with a satisfactory text-book. The course I would recommend for such students comprises all that precedes the Appendix, except the bracketed portions. Those teachers who have not time to go over so much ground will find it possible to omit also §§ **7, 8, 13, 15, 17, 18**, and **43**, and perhaps some other sections. Those, on the other hand, who are able to exceed the course described above are advised to take up the table of Logarithms of Sums and Differences.

Only the rudiments of the theory of logarithms

are required at the examination, but candidates are expected to be thoroughly drilled in practical work. Applicants in Course II., however, should be well prepared on all the unbracketed parts of the book, including the Appendix. The use of the trigonometric tables is not required for admission in Course I.

I would further respectfully ask the attention of professors of mathematics in other colleges to the desirableness of putting into the hands of students tables of three or four places instead of the bulky volumes which even practical computers need for only the more delicate kinds of work, and especially instead of the inconvenient and poorly constructed tables often found bound up in the same covers with a work on trigonometry. This has been pointed out by several of the best authorities abroad, and is, no doubt, widely acknowledged here as well. I venture to hope, therefore, that the publication of this little treatise will induce a more general employment of the tables to which it is designed as a companion.

J. M. PEIRCE.

CAMBRIDGE, *October* 1873.

CONTENTS.

	PAGE
CHAPTER I. — GENERAL PRINCIPLES	1
CHAPTER II. — THE DENARY SYSTEM	17
CHAPTER III. — COMPUTATION BY LOGARITHMS	26
Table of Proportional Parts	37
Three-Place Table of Logarithms of Numbers	38
Four-Place Table of Logarithms of Numbers	39
Arithmetical Complement. Reciprocal	43
Multiplication by Logarithms	44
Division by Logarithms	45
The Rule of Three by Logarithms	46
Involution by Logarithms	46
Evolution by Logarithms	47
Compound Operations	48
Exponential Equations	48
Logarithms of Sums and Differences	49
APPENDIX. — EXPLANATION OF THE TRIGONOMETRIC TABLES	55
Three-Place Table of Trigonometric Functions	56
Four-Place Table of Logarithmic Trigonometric Functions	63
Inverse Trigonometric Functions	69
Examples in Trigonometry adapted to the Four-Place Tables	76

THE
ELEMENTS OF LOGARITHMS.

CHAPTER I.

GENERAL PRINCIPLES.

§ 1. Logarithms are numbers that are substituted in computation for other numbers, to which they bear such a relation that the operations to be performed on the latter are represented by simpler operations performed on the former. The method of logarithms was first propounded in 1614, in a book entitled *Mirifici Logarithmorum Canonis Descriptio*, by JOHN NAPIER (latinized *Nepĕrus*), Baron of Merchiston in Scotland, who was born about 1550, and died in 1618, four years after the publication of his memorable invention. This method has contributed very powerfully to the modern advance of science, and especially of astronomy, by facilitating the laborious calculations without which that advance could not have been made. It is also constantly employed in surveying, navigation, and other branches of practical mathematics; and it may be used with much advantage in all multiplications and divisions of numbers of three or more figures.

Besides their usefulness in computation, logarithms fill an important place in the higher theoretical mathematics; but, in this book, we shall consider them almost wholly in their practical aspect.

The word *logarithm*, which is due to Napier himself, is formed from λόγος, *ratio*, and ἀριθμός, *number*, and means *a number that indicates a ratio*. It refers to the proposition, which will be proved in its proper place, and which was made by Napier his fundamental theorem, that the difference of two logarithms determines the ratio of the numbers for which they stand, so that an arithmetical series of logarithms corresponds to a geometric series of numbers.

§ 2. The **base** of a system of logarithms is *a fixed number* to which all numbers are referred in that system. It may have *any positive value except unity*.

The **logarithm** of a number in any system is *the exponent of the power to which the base of the system must be raised to produce that number*.

The **antilogarithm** of a number is *that number of which the given number is the logarithm;* in other words, it is *that power of the base of which the given number is the exponent*.

Thus, in a system of logarithms of which 8 is the base,

$$\log\ 8 = 1, \quad \text{antilog } 1 = 8,$$
$$\log\ 64 = 2, \quad \text{antilog } 2 = 64,$$
$$\log\ 512 = 3, \quad \text{antilog } 3 = 512,$$
$$\log\ 4096 = 4, \&c., \quad \text{antilog } 4 = 4096, \&c.$$

In general, if x and u have any such values as to satisfy the equation

$$a^u = x,$$

we have, in the system of which a is the base,

$$u = \log x, \quad x = \text{antilog } u;$$

and either of the two latter equations may be regarded as equivalent to the former.

Napier at first called logarithms *artificial numbers*, and antilogarithms *natural numbers;* and the latter designation is still often used. The word *antilogarithm* is modern; and, though a convenient term, is used by a few writers only.

§ 3. The following formulas are proved in algebra, and the proofs, which are readily derived from the principle that the exponent of a quantity denotes **the number of times the quantity is taken as a factor** in the term into which it enters, should here be given by the student: —

$$a^u \, a^v \, a^w \ldots \ldots = a^{u+v+w+\cdots}, \quad (1)$$

$$\frac{a^u}{a^v} = a^{u-v}, \quad (2)$$

$$(a^u)^v = a^{uv}, \quad (3)$$

$$\sqrt[v]{a^u} = a^{\frac{u}{v}}. \quad (4)$$

§ 4. The following principles are less familiar: —
If, in (2), $u = v$,

$$\frac{a^u}{a^v} = 1, \qquad a^{u-v} = a^0;$$

$$\therefore \quad a^0 = 1; \quad (5)$$

that is, the **zero** power of *any quantity* is **unity**. This result conforms to the principle cited in § 3. For to introduce any quantity into a term *zero times* as a factor is equivalent to introducing *unity* as a factor, since either of these operations would leave the term unchanged. That is, $a^0 b = b$, since b is multiplied by a zero times, and also $1 b = b$; so that $a^0 b = 1 b$, or $a^0 = 1$.

If, in (2), $u = 0$, then, by (5) and (2),

$$\frac{a^u}{a^v} = \frac{1}{a^v}, \qquad a^{u-v} = a^{-v};$$

$$\therefore \quad a^{-v} = \frac{1}{a^v}; \quad (6)$$

that is, a quantity with a **negative exponent** denotes the **reciprocal*** of the same quantity with *the corresponding positive exponent.* Thus, $8^{-2} = \frac{1}{64}$. This result may also be brought into conformity with the principle of § 3. For to divide by a^v, or to multiply by $\frac{1}{a^v}$, is to *take away* a as a factor v times; that is, to take it v times *less* than before; and this is precisely what must be meant by taking it $(-v)$ times *more* than before. Hence $\frac{1}{a^v}$ is the same thing as a^{-v}.

If, in (4), u is not divisible by v, the **fractional exponent** may still be used to denote the operation of successively raising to **the power denoted by the numerator** and extracting **the root denoted by the denominator.** Thus, $8^{\frac{2}{3}} = \sqrt[3]{8^2} = 4$, $8^{-\frac{2}{3}} = \frac{1}{4}$. This result, again, is conformable to our general principle. For $\sqrt[v]{a^u}$ is that quantity which, taken v times as a factor, gives a taken u times as a factor. We may then regard it as a taken $\frac{u}{v}$ times as a factor, and hence write $\sqrt[v]{a^u} = a^{\frac{u}{v}}$.

Exponents may then be either positive, negative, or null, and may be either integral or fractional. They may even be *incommensurable*,† for the value of a power having an incommensurable exponent can be found, within any required limits of error, by taking a sufficiently approximate fractional value of the exponent.

---

* The *reciprocal* of a quantity is the quotient obtained by dividing unity by that quantity; e.g., the reciprocal of x is $\frac{1}{x}$.

† Two quantities are said to be *incommensurable to each other*, when they have no common measure. A number is called *incommensurable*, when it is incommensurable to *unity*, and therefore cannot be exactly expressed by an integer, or by the ratio of two integers; i.e., by a fraction. Circulating decimals must not be confounded with incommensurable numbers. Thus, $\sqrt{2}$ is incommensurable, but $0.\dot{6}$ is not incommensurable. The ratio of two quantities incommensurable to each other is an incommensurable number. An incommensurable number can be expressed fractionally *within any required limit of accuracy.* Thus, 1.4142 expresses $\sqrt{2}$ within ±0.00005. Incommensurable numbers are also called *surds*.

It is easily proved that formulas (1-4) hold for *any values of the exponents*. For we have shown that *the general principle from which those formulas are derived may be extended to all exponents*. For example, we have

$$\frac{\sqrt{a}}{\sqrt[3]{a}\sqrt[4]{a}} = a^{\frac{1}{2}} a^{-\frac{1}{3}} a^{-\frac{1}{4}} = a^{-\frac{1}{12}} = \frac{1}{\sqrt[12]{a}}.$$

§ 5. *Since any number may be an exponent,* **any number may be a logarithm.**

Thus, if 8 is the base,

$$8^{-2} = \tfrac{1}{64}, \qquad 8^{\frac{2}{3}} = 4, \qquad 8^{-\frac{2}{3}} = \tfrac{1}{4}.$$
$$\therefore -2 = \log \tfrac{1}{64}, \quad \tfrac{2}{3} = \log 4, \quad -\tfrac{2}{3} = \log \tfrac{1}{4}.$$

§ 6. Since $a^0 = 1$, therefore,

in any system, $\log 1 = 0, \quad \text{antilog } 0 = 1.$ (7)

Since $a^1 = a$, therefore,

in any system, $\log \text{base} = 1, \quad \text{antilog } 1 = \text{base.}$ (8)

By (6), if a is the base,

$$\log \frac{1}{a^u} = -u = -\log a^u;\qquad(9)$$

or *the logarithm of the reciprocal of any number in any system is equal to the negative of the logarithm of the number in the same system.*

If $a > 1$, the result obtained by taking it as a factor an infinite number of times is itself infinite; so that

$$a^{+\infty} = \infty, \; a^{-\infty} = \frac{1}{a^{+\infty}} = \frac{1}{\infty} = 0.*$$

---

* If x increases indefinitely, $\frac{1}{x}$ decreases indefinitely; and if x decreases indefinitely, $\frac{1}{x}$ increases indefinitely. Hence

$$\frac{1}{\infty} = 0, \quad \frac{1}{0} = \infty.$$

$$\therefore \log \infty = +\infty, \quad \text{antilog}(+\infty) = \infty,$$
$$\log 0 = -\infty, \quad \text{antilog}(-\infty) = 0.$$
$$\} \ (10)$$

If $a < 1$, $a^{-1} > 1$, and hence

$$(a^{-1})^{+\infty} = a^{-\infty} = \infty, \ a^{+\infty} = \frac{1}{a^{-\infty}} = \frac{1}{\infty} = 0.$$

$$\therefore \log \infty = -\infty, \quad \text{antilog}(+\infty) = 0,$$
$$\log 0 = +\infty, \quad \text{antilog}(-\infty) = \infty.$$
$$\} \ (11)$$

§ 7. If the base is greater than unity (as is the case in the common systems), its positive integral powers are all greater than unity, and their reciprocals, the negative integral powers, are, consequently, all less than unity. For example, $5^3 > 1$, $5^{-3} < 1$, &c.

Any fractional power of the base, $a^{\frac{m}{n}}$, is, in like manner, greater or less than unity, according as its nth power, a^m, is greater or less than unity (provided n is positive); and a^m is greater or less than unity, according as m is positive or negative; that is, according as the original exponent $\frac{m}{n}$ is positive or negative. Hence, all the positive powers of the base (both integral and fractional) are greater than unity, and all the negative powers are less than unity; so that, *if the base is greater than unity, the logarithms of all numbers greater than unity are positive, and the logarithms of all numbers less than unity are negative.*

It is shown in the same way that, *if the base is less than unity, the logarithms of all numbers less than unity are positive, and the logarithms of all numbers greater than unity are negative.*

Thus, if 8 is the base, $\log 4 = +\frac{2}{3}$, $\log \frac{1}{4} = -\frac{2}{3}$; but if $\frac{1}{8}$ is the base, $\log 4 = -\frac{2}{3}$, $\log \frac{1}{4} = +\frac{2}{3}$.

§ 8. If x and $(x + h)$ are two numbers, and u and $(u + k)$ their logarithms, then
$x = a^u$, $x + h = a^{u+k} = a^u a^k$ by (1), $h = a^u(a^k - 1)$.

If then $x+h > x$; that is, if h is positive; a^k must be greater than 1; so that, by § 7, if $a > 1$, k is positive, and $u + k > u$, but if $a < 1$, k is negative, and $u + k < u$.

Hence, *the greater of two numbers has the greater logarithm in a system of which the base is greater than unity, and the less logarithm in a system of which the base is less than unity.*

Thus, if 8 is the base, log $8 >$ log 4; but if $\frac{1}{8}$ is the base, log $8 <$ log 4.

[§ **9**.* We have seen that $a^u = 1$, if $u = 0$, and that a^u differs from 1, if u differs from 0. But it is possible to make the difference between a^u and 1 *less than any quantity that may be assigned* by making u sufficiently small.

For if m is any value of u (positive, if $a > 1$; negative, if $a < 1$), and if $a^m = p > 1$, then if we reduce the value of u to $\frac{1}{2}m$, $x = a^{\frac{1}{2}m} = p^{\frac{1}{2}} = \sqrt{p}$. Now, by the principle $a^2 - b^2 = (a+b)(a-b)$,

$$\sqrt{p} - 1 = \frac{p-1}{\sqrt{p+1}}.$$

But since $p > 1$, $\sqrt{p} + 1 > 2$.

$$\therefore \sqrt{p} - 1 < \tfrac{1}{2}(p-1).$$

Hence, by halving the value of u, the difference $(x-1)$ is reduced to an amount *less than half* its former value. Now we can successively halve the value of u as many times as we please, and if $(x-1)$ were halved at the same time, we could, by carrying the process far enough, make that difference less than any assigned quantity; then we can certainly accomplish this, when $(x-1)$ is reduced *more rapidly* than by successive halving.

We have seen that if $x > 1$, we can find a value of u that will make $(x-1)$ as small as we please. Then the

---

* Sections included in brackets may be omitted by the beginner.

reciprocal of x, which is less than 1, can be made to differ from 1 as little as we please, since

$$1 - \tfrac{1}{x} = \tfrac{x-1}{x} < x - 1.$$

But the value of u for $\tfrac{1}{x}$ is the *negative* of the value of u for x. See (9).

Hence, by making the logarithm sufficiently near 0, and either positive or negative, *we can bring the antilogarithm as near 1 as we please, making it at the same time either greater or less than 1 at our discretion.*]

[§ **10.** If x and $(x + h)$ are two numbers, and u and $(u + k)$ their logarithms, then, as in § **8**,

$$h = a^u (a^k - 1) = x (a^k - 1).$$

But, by making k sufficiently small, we can, by § **9**, make $(a^k - 1)$ as small as we please, and therefore small enough to render h less than any quantity that may be assigned. Hence, by making a sufficiently small change in the value of a logarithm, we can make the corresponding change in the antilogarithm as small as we please; and if the logarithm increases *continuously* (that is, by insensible gradations) from $-\infty$ to $+\infty$, *the antilogarithm will also change its value continuously; increasing from 0 to $+\infty$, if the base is greater than unity; and decreasing from $+\infty$ to 0, if the base is less than unity; and, in either case, passing through every intermediate value.*

We see then that, *in any system of logarithms, every positive number has one and only one real logarithm*, and conversely that *every real number (positive or negative) has one and only one antilogarithm, which is always positive.*

Negative numbers have no real logarithms, and when they occur in logarithmic calculations, the *arithmetical value* of the number and its *sign* must be considered separately.]

[§ **11.** The word *real* is used in the last article in a technical sense, which is likely to be new to the student. *Real quantities*, or *reals*, are whole numbers, ratios between whole numbers (that is, fractions), and incommensurable numbers (which can be approximately represented by fractions), and are either positive or negative; that is to say, they are the ordinary quantities of arithmetic and elementary algebra. Distinguished from them are *imaginary quantities* or *imaginaries*. Of these algebra affords examples in the *even roots of negative quantities* (such as $\sqrt{-1}$), which cannot be real, since no real quantity produces a negative result when raised to an even power. In the elementary mathematics, imaginaries appear merely as absurd expressions, to which little attention is paid; but in the higher study of the relations of quantity, they assume great importance. In the higher theory of logarithms, it is found that every number (whether positive, negative, or imaginary) has, in any system, *an infinity of logarithms*, which are, in general, all imaginary; but that *if the number is real and positive, one and only one of its logarithms is real*, and this is the logarithm ordinarily considered.

Imaginary logarithms cannot be made use of in practical computation, and we shall not have occasion to consider them further. We only refer to them here in order to explain why we have so carefully guarded the language of the foregoing article.]

[§ **12.** We have said that a real logarithm has but one antilogarithm, which is always positive. Other values of the antilogarithm might also be admitted. For example, since $a^{\frac{1}{2}} = \sqrt{a}$ has two values, we might consider antilog 0.5 as having two values, one positive and the other negative. But mathematicians have found it best to admit *only one value of the antilogarithm*, even in that higher theory of logarithms to which allusion has just been made; and in the exponential equation

$$a^u = x,$$

x is regarded as having but one value for each value of u, and as being *real and positive* whenever u is *real*, assuming a to be real and positive.]

§ 13. If several logarithms form an arithmetical progression, their antilogarithms form a geometric progression.

For if the logarithms are

$$u,\ u+k,\ u+2k,\ u+3k,\ \ldots\ldots\ldots$$

and if we denote a^u by x, and a^k by h, the antilogarithms of the given logarithms will be, by (1) and (3),

$$x,\ hx,\ h^2x,\ h^3x,\ \ldots\ldots$$

It will be observed that k, the *constant difference* in the series of logarithms, is the logarithm of h, the *constant ratio* in the series of antilogarithms.

Example. In the system of which 8 is the base,

$$\begin{aligned}
\text{antilog } 4 &= 4096, \\
\text{antilog } 3\tfrac{1}{3} &= 1024, \\
\text{antilog } 2\tfrac{2}{3} &= 256, \\
\text{antilog } 2 &= 64, \\
\text{antilog } 1\tfrac{1}{3} &= 16, \\
\text{antilog } \tfrac{2}{3} &= 4, \\
\text{antilog } 0 &= 1, \\
\text{antilog } (-\tfrac{2}{3}) &= \tfrac{1}{4}, \\
\text{antilog } (-1\tfrac{1}{3}) &= \tfrac{1}{16}, \\
\text{antilog } (-2) &= \tfrac{1}{64},\ \&\text{c}.
\end{aligned}$$

Here $k = -\tfrac{2}{3}$, $h = \tfrac{1}{4} = \text{antilog } (-\tfrac{2}{3})$.

GENERAL PRINCIPLES. 11

[§ **14.** *The terms of any arithmetical progression of which one term is* 0 *may be considered as logarithms of the corresponding terms of any geometric progression of which one term is* 1; those terms being regarded as corresponding which are similarly situated relatively to the terms 0 and 1 respectively, and the *base* of the system being *that root of the constant ratio of the latter series of which the exponent is the constant difference of the former series.*

Let $k =$ the constant difference of the arithmetical progression,

$h =$ the constant ratio of the geometric progression.

Then mk and h^m will denote any two corresponding terms of the two series, and if we take a, the base of the system, such that

$$a = \sqrt[k]{h} = h^{\frac{1}{k}}, \text{ or } a^k = h, \text{ or } a^{mk} = h^m,$$

we have

$$k = \log h, \qquad mk = \log h^m;$$

which proves the proposition, and shows that the constant difference of the arithmetical series is the logarithm of the constant ratio of the geometric series.]

§ **15.** Let u, u', and u'' be three successive logarithms in the series of § 13, and x, x', and x'' their antilogarithms. Then

$$u'' - u' = u' - u = k, \; x' - x = (h-1)x,$$
$$x'' - x' = (h-1)\,hx = h\,(x'-x).$$

If now k be taken very near 0, h will be very near 1, since $h = a^k$; and consequently

$$(x'' - x') = (x' - x) \text{ approximately};$$

that is, *if the successive differences of three logarithms are* **equal and very small,** *the differences of their antilogarithms are* **approximately equal.**

Hence it follows that *if the successive differences of three logarithms are* **very small** *and not equal, the differences of their antilogarithms are* **approximately proportional** *to those of the logarithms.* For if the successive differences of the logarithms be divided into equal parts, those of the antilogarithms will be divided into the same number of parts, which will be approximately equal.

We do not here stop to inquire *how* small the differences must be in order that the error resulting from the application of this theorem may remain within definite limits. That is a question which requires for its answer higher principles of logarithms than those explained in this chapter. The theorem itself is, however, necessary in the practical use of logarithms.

§ **16.** We have now considered the general nature of logarithms. Their utility in computation is derived from the following theorems:—

I. **The logarithm of the continued product of several quantities is the sum of their logarithms.**

II. **The logarithm of the quotient of two quantities is the excess of the logarithm of the dividend over that of the divisor.**

III. **The logarithm of any power of a quantity is the product obtained by multiplying the logarithm of the quantity by the exponent of the power.**

IV. **The logarithm of any root of a quantity is the quotient obtained by dividing the logarithm of the quantity by the exponent of the root.**

These theorems are also conveniently stated in the following formulas:—

I. $\log (xyz\ldots\ldots) = \log x + \log y + \log z + \ldots\ldots$, (12)

which may be written, if Σ is used for the word *sum*, and Π for the word *product*,

GENERAL PRINCIPLES.

I. $\quad\log \Pi x = \Sigma \log x.$ (13)

II. $\quad\log \dfrac{x}{y} = \log x - \log y.$ (14)

III. $\quad\log x^n = n \log x.$ (15)

IV. $\quad\log \sqrt[n]{x} = \dfrac{1}{n} \log x.$ (16)

The proofs of these theorems are easily derived from formulas (1–4).

I. Let $u = \log x$, $v = \log y$, $w = \log z$, &c.

Then, if a is the base of the system,

$$x = a^u,\ y = a^v,\ z = a^w,\ \&c.$$

Then, by (1),

$$xyz\ldots = a^{u+v+w+\cdots},$$

or $\quad \Pi x = a^{\Sigma u}.$

∴ by § 2, $\log \Pi x = \Sigma u = \Sigma \log x.$

II. With the same notation, by (2),

$$\dfrac{x}{y} = a^{u-v}.$$

∴ by § 2, $\log \dfrac{x}{y} = u - v = \log x - \log y.$

III. With the same notation, by (3),

$$x^n = a^{nu}.$$

∴ by § 2, $\log x^n = nu = n \log x,$

where it should be observed that n may be positive or negative, integral or fractional.

IV. With the same notation, by (4),

$$\sqrt[n]{x} = a^{\frac{u}{n}}.$$

∴ by § 2, $\log \sqrt[n]{x} = \dfrac{u}{n} = \dfrac{1}{n} \log x.$

These theorems show that the use of logarithms enables us to replace the operations of multiplication, division, involution, and evolution, by operations respectively simpler.

Multiplication is replaced by *Addition*.
Division is replaced by *Subtraction*.
Involution is replaced by *Multiplication*.
Evolution is replaced by *Division*.

§ 17. *The logarithms of proportional numbers are equidifferent.*

For the proportion
$$\frac{m}{n} = \frac{p}{q}$$
gives, by (14),
$$\log m - \log n = \log p - \log q; \qquad (17)$$
whence is derived the following formula for the logarithm of the fourth term of a proportion,
$$\log q = \log p + \log n - \log m. \qquad (18)$$

This proposition is given by Napier as the *First Proposition* of the theory of logarithms.

§ 18. An **exponential equation** is easily solved by means of logarithms.

For let the equation be
$$b^x = m,$$
where x is the unknown quantity, and b and m are positive. Then, by (15),
$$\log m = \log b^x = x \log b.$$
$$\therefore x = \frac{\log m}{\log b}. \qquad (19)$$

[§ **19**. If b be made the base of a system of logarithms, then, by § 2, $x = \log m$ in the system of which b is the base. We obtain, then, from (19) the following theorem: —

If the logarithm of a number in any system be divided by the logarithm of a second number in the same system, the quotient is the logarithm of the first number in a new system, of which the second number is the base.

When logarithms belonging to different systems are brought into the same formula, it is convenient to distinguish them by writing the symbol of the base as a *suffix* to the symbol "log." Thus,

$\log_a m = \log m$ in the system of which a is the base,
$\log_b m = \log m$ .... b ....;
and we have

$$\log_b m = \frac{\log_a m}{\log_a b}. \quad] \qquad (20)$$

[§ **20**. If $m = a$, $\log_a m = 1$, by (8), and (20) becomes

$$\log_b a = \frac{1}{\log_a b}, \text{ or } \log_a b . \log_b a = 1; \qquad (21)$$

so that, when we change from one system of logarithms to another, *the logarithm of the old base in the new system is the reciprocal of the logarithm of the new base in the old system.*]

[§ **21**. Combining (20) and (21), we have

$$\log_b m = \log_b a . \log_a m.] \qquad (22)$$

[§ **22**. We see, by (20) and (22), that, if the logarithms of a series of numbers are computed in any system, we can convert them to any other system, by dividing all the computed logarithms by one fixed quantity, namely the logarithm of the new base in old system, or by multiplying all the computed logarithms by one fixed quantity, namely the logarithm of the old base in the new system.

Thus, a system of logarithms founded on the base 8 can be converted into a system of which $\frac{1}{2}$ is the base, by multiplying the logarithms of the former system by -3, which equals log 8 in the latter system (since $(\frac{1}{2})^{-3} = 8$); as will be seen by the following table:

Nos.	logs (base 8)	logs (base $\frac{1}{2}$)
4096,	4,	$-12,$
1024,	$3\frac{1}{3},$	$-10,$
256,	$2\frac{2}{3},$	$-8,$
64,	2,	$-6,$
16,	$1\frac{1}{3},$	$-4,$
8,	1,	$-3,$
4,	$\frac{2}{3},$	$-2,$
2,	$\frac{1}{3},$	$-1,$
1,	0,	0,
$\frac{1}{2},$	$-\frac{1}{3},$	1,
$\frac{1}{4},$	$-\frac{2}{3},$	2,
$\frac{1}{8},$	$-1,$	3,
$\frac{1}{16},$	$-1\frac{1}{3},$	4.]

CHAPTER II.

THE DENARY SYSTEM.

§ 23. There is an infinite variety of possible systems of logarithms; but only three have been actually used by mathematicians. These are the system of *Napier*, the *natural* system, and the *denary* system.

The **denary**, or *decimal*, system is that which has the number 10 for its base. In practical computation, it is far more convenient than any other, and is now used exclusively, on account of its relation to the ordinary numeral system of arithmetic. It was proposed in 1617 by HENRY BRIGGS, then Professor of Geometry in Gresham College, London, and afterwards Savilian Professor of Geometry at Oxford. This mathematician was among the first to recognize the importance of the invention of logarithms, and he made two journeys to Scotland for the purpose of visiting Napier, in consultation with whom he formed his new system, — a system distinguished from the original one not only in being founded on the number 10, but also in some important simplifications of theory.

Denary logarithms are sometimes called *Briggsian*, and sometimes *common*, or *vulgar*.

The *natural* system, though not so well adapted to use in computation as the denary, is the most important of all systems in the higher theory of logarithms. It may be regarded as a modification of the system of Napier, with which it is often erroneously confounded. But the *original Neperian* system was immediately superseded by that of Briggs, with the approval of Napier himself, and now has only an historical interest.

[§ **24**. It is a principle of the Theory of Numbers that a composite number can be resolved into prime factors in only one way. If then m is any positive integer, $10^m = 2^m 5^m$ can only be formed of m 2's and m 5's. If, again, n is any positive integer not a divisor of m, $\sqrt[n]{10^m} = 10^{\frac{m}{n}}$ cannot be an integer. For the prime factors of such an integer must be divisors of 10^m and must therefore be a certain number of 2's and 5's, which repeated n times would give m 2's and m 5's; but this is impossible, since n is not a divisor of m. Again, $\sqrt[n]{10^m}$ cannot be a commensurable fraction irreducible to an integer. For the nth power of such a fraction would itself be a fraction irreducible to an integer. Moreover, $10^{-\frac{m}{n}}$ can be neither an integer nor a commensurable fraction; for, if it were, its reciprocal, $10^{\frac{m}{n}}$ would be commensurable. Hence, if u is a commensurable irreducible fraction (positive or negative), 10^u is incommensurable; and hence, conversely if 10^u is commensurable, u is incommensurable, if it is not an integer. *In the denary system, then, the logarithms of all commensurable numbers, except the integral powers of* 10, *are incommensurable, and the antilogarithms of all commensurable fractional logarithms are incommensurable.*]

§ **25**. The denary logarithm of any number is either an integer, or else consists of an integer (which may be 0) *plus* a fraction, which is customarily expressed decimally to a greater or less number of places. The integral part of the logarithm is called its **characteristic**, and the decimal part its **mantissa**. Thus the characteristic of the logarithm 1.6875 .. is 1, and its mantissa is .6875 ..;

the characteristic of 0.3010.. is 0, and its mantissa is .3010...

§ 26. The *significant figures* of any number are those figures that remain when all zeros at the beginning and end of the number are omitted. Thus, the significant figures of the numbers 81004000, 81004, 810.04, and 0.081004, are 81004.

It will be seen that *zero* is a significant figure, when it occurs *between other significant figures*, so that it cannot be omitted without changing their relative numeral position.

§ 27. If two numbers consist of the same series of significant figures, their logarithms, in the denary system, have the same mantissa, and the difference of their characteristics is equal to the number of numeral places by which the units' place of one number is removed from the units' place of the other.

For it is a principle of arithmetical numeration that the operation of moving the units' place in any number n places is equivalent to multiplying the number by $10^{\pm n}$, the exponent being positive if the units' place is moved to the right, negative if it is moved to the left. But to multiply a number by $10^{\pm n}$ is, by (13), equivalent to adding the integer $\pm n$ to its logarithm; and this addition does not affect the mantissa of the logarithm, but increases or diminishes its characteristic by n, the number of places by which the units' place has been removed.

Thus, if we know that
$$\log 48.7 = 1.6875..,$$
it follows that
$$\log 48700 = 4.6875..,$$
$$\log 4.87 = 0.6875..,$$
$$\log 0.00487 = -3 + .6875..$$
$$= -2.3125...$$

20   THE ELEMENTS OF LOGARITHMS.

The above theorem expresses the fundamental property of the denary system, on which the peculiar utility of that system depends.

§ **28.** In any system of logarithms, $\log 1 = 0$, by (7). We have, then, in the denary system, by § **27**,

$$\begin{aligned}
\log 10 &= 1, & \log 0.1 &= -1 \\
\log 100 &= 2, & \log 0.01 &= -2 \\
\log 1000 &= 3, & \log 0.001 &= -3 \\
\log 10000 &= 4, & \log 0.0001 &= -4 \\
\&c., & & \&c.,
\end{aligned} \quad (23)$$

that is, *the logarithm of a number which consists of a single figure* 1 *and cyphers is an integer, and is equal to the number of places by which the units' place is removed from the figure* 1, being *positive or negative*, according as the units' place is on the *right or left* of the figure 1, and *null* if 1 is *in* the units' place.

The principle of numeration referred to in § **27** shows that the numbers here spoken of are *the integral powers of* 10; that is, that

$$\begin{aligned}
10^1 &= 10, & 10^{-1} &= 0.1, \\
10^2 &= 100, & 10^{-2} &= 0.01, \\
\&c., & & \&c.,
\end{aligned}$$

and (23) may also be obtained directly from these equations, by the definition of a logarithm, § **2**.

§ **29.** Any positive number is either an integral power of 10, or else it lies between two successive integral powers, of which the lower contains the figure 1 in the same numeral place as the first significant figure of the given number, and the higher contains the figure 1 in the next place to the left. For example,

$$\begin{aligned}
10 &< 48.7 < 100, \\
0.001 &< 0.00487 < 0.01, \\
&\&c.
\end{aligned}$$

Then, by § 8, the logarithm of a number which is not an integral power of 10 lies between the two successive integers which are the logarithms of the integral powers determined as above; and it is therefore equal to the *less* of those two integers *plus* a fractional quantity less than 1. The latter quantity is the *mantissa* of the logarithm; the integer is the *characteristic* of the logarithm.

Hence, *the* **characteristic** *of the logarithm of any number, in the denary system, is equal to* **the number of places by which the units' place is removed from the first significant figure**, being *positive* if the units' place is on the *right* of the first significant figure (that is, if the number > 10), *negative* if it is on the left (that is, if the number < 1), and *null* if the first significant figure is *in* the units' place (that is, if the number is between 1 and 10).

Thus,

characteristic of log $48700 = 4$,
characteristic of log $4870 = 3$,
characteristic of log $487 = 2$,
characteristic of log $48.7 = 1$,
characteristic of log $4.87 = 0$,
characteristic of log $0.487 = -1$,
characteristic of log $0.0487 = -2$,
characteristic of log $0.00487 = -3$,
&c., &c.

§ 30. The above rule for determining the characteristic makes it necessary that that which is added to the characteristic to produce the logarithm, that is, the *mantissa*, shall be *positive in all cases*, even when the logarithm, as a whole, is negative. Thus, log 0.00487 is between -3 and -2, and we have seen (in § 27) that it is either

$$-3 + .6875..\quad \text{or} \quad -2 - .3125..$$

But our rule makes the characteristic -3, and therefore

necessitates the adoption of the first of these forms. In order to avoid writing the sign $+$ between the characteristic and mantissa, we write the sign $-$ *over* the characteristic, as a way of indicating that it affects that figure only. For example, we write

$$\log 0.00487 = \overline{3}.6875 \ldots$$

But as negative characteristics are often a source of confusion in computation, it is customary to *add* 10 *to every negative characteristic*, and to write $-$ 10 after the logarithm. Thus we have

$$\log 0.00487 = 7.6875 \ldots - 10.$$

The $-$ 10 is often omitted in writing, and left to be remembered.

There is sometimes no advantage in adding 10 to the negative characteristic; but the student is advised to use this method in all cases, for the sake of having a fixed rule.

§ **31.** The *characteristic* of a logarithm depends, as we see, wholly on the position of the units' place in the antilogarithm, and not at all on the significant figures which compose it. This part of the logarithm is then readily found by inspection of the number. The *mantissa*, on the other hand, can only be obtained by laborious calculations, and the practical computer must consult his table for it. But this part of the logarithm depends entirely on the series of significant figures that compose the antilogarithm, without regard to the position of the units' place. Hence, if a table is so made as to give the logarithm of *any number between two successive integral powers of* 10, as 100 and 1000, it will give the logarithm of *any number whatever*, since all possible series of significant figures can be found within the chosen limits. This is a great advantage which the denary system of logarithms has over any other.

But we can suppose *an infinity* of numbers between any two given numbers, as 100 and 1000, and it is impossible that the logarithms of all these numbers should be explicitly contained in any table. They can only be given at certain intervals; but if these intervals are made sufficiently small, the logarithms of intermediate numbers can be found from the table by a process called *interpolation*, which is founded on the principle of § 15, and will be fully explained in the next chapter. The greater the degree of accuracy with which the logarithm is required, the smaller should be the ratio of the intervals, in the table, to the numbers which are separated by those intervals. Thus, a table of *four-place* logarithms may be limited to the logarithms of all integers from 100 to 1000, where the above-named ratio has for its greatest value $\frac{1}{100}$; while a *seven-place* table should include the logarithm of every integer from 10,000 to 100,000, where the greatest value of the ratio is $\frac{1}{10000}$.

[§ **32.** We are indebted to Briggs, not only as the author of the denary system, but also as the founder, and, in great part, the computer of the tables now actually used. In 1617, he published the first instalment of his own table, containing the logarithms of all integers below 1000 to *eight* places of decimals; and this he followed, in 1624, by his *Arithmetica Logarithmica*, containing the logarithms of all integers from 1 to 20,000 and from 90,000 100,000 to *fourteen* places of decimals, together with a learned introduction, in which the theory and use of logarithms are fully developed. The interval from 20,000 to 90,000 was filled up by ADRIAN VLACQ, a Dutch computer; but in his table, which appeared in 1628, the logarithms were given to only *ten* places of decimals.

"The total number of errors found in Vlacq," says Mr. Glaisher, "amounts to 603, which probably includes very nearly all that exist; this cannot be regarded as a great number, when it is considered that the table was the result of an original calculation, and that more than 2,100,000 printed figures are liable to error." (*Athenæum*, 15 June 1872. See also the *Monthly Notices of the Royal Astronomical Society* for May, 1872.) All the modern published tables are founded on that of Vlacq, of which an edition, containing many corrections, was issued at Leipzig in 1794 under the title *Thesaurus Logarithmorum Completus* by *George Vega*. Concerning Vega's table Professor De Morgan writes, "This is, no doubt, up to this time, *the* table of logarithms; the one of all others to which ultimate reference should be made in questions of accuracy." (*English Cyclopædia, Arts and Sciences*, Vol. VII., article " Table," London, 1861.)

Callet's seven-place table (Paris, 1795), instead of stopping at 100,000, gives the eight-place logarithms of the numbers between 100,000 and 108,000, in order to diminish the errors of interpolation, which are greatest in the early part of the table; and this addition has been since generally included in seven-place tables. But the only important published extension of Vlacq's table has been made by Mr. Sang (1871), whose table contains the seven-place logarithms of all numbers below 200,000.

Briggs and Vlacq also published original tables of the logarithms of the trigonometric functions.

Besides the tables we have named, we ought to mention the great collection, called *Tables du Cadastre*, which was constructed under the direction of *Prony*, by an original computation, under the auspices of the French republican government of the last century. This work, which contains, besides other tables, the logarithms of all numbers up to 100,000 to nineteen places, and of the numbers between 100,000 and 200,000 to twenty-four places, exists only in manuscript, "in seventeen enormous folios," at the Observatory of Paris. It was begun in 1792 (year ii.); and "the whole of the calculations, which to secure greater accuracy were performed in duplicate, and the two manuscripts subsequently collated with care, were completed in the short space of two years." (*English Cyclopædia, Biography*, Vol. IV., article "Prony.")

For further information on the subject of this section, and for an enumeration and description of tables published up to 1861, the student is referred to the article "Table" in the *English Cyclopædia* already cited.]

CHAPTER III.

COMPUTATION BY LOGARITHMS.

§ 33. This chapter on the practical use of logarithms is adapted to the author's *Three and Four Place Tables of Logarithmic and Trigonometric Functions.*

§ 34. Quantities are divided into two classes: **constants** and **variables**; and variables are divided into two classes: **independent variables** and **functions**.

A *constant* is a quantity which is conceived to be restricted to one or more fixed values; a *variable* is a quantity which is not so restricted, and (in general) may have any value.

When the value of a variable is regarded as being assumed arbitrarily, the variable is called an *independent variable;* when it is regarded as being determined by the values of other variables, the variable is called a *function* of the variables by which it is determined.

The independent variables which enter into any question are often called simply *the variables.*

If, for instance, in the equation $a^u = x$, a denotes the base of a definite system of logarithms, while x denotes *any* number, and u its logarithm, a is a constant, and x and u are variables, either of which may be regarded as an independent variable, and the other as a function of it. But if a is variable, as well as x and u, any two of the three quantities may be regarded as independent variables, and the third as a function of those two. Thus, a function may depend on only one independent variable or on any number of independent variables.

A logarithm in a given system may be regarded as a function of its antilogarithm, or an antilogarithm as a function of its logarithm. But we shall generally consider the relation in the former light, and speak of the antilogarithm as the independent variable, and of its logarithm as a function of that variable; and in that case we shall commonly use the equation

$$u = \log x,$$

in which we shall call x the independent variable and u a function of x. When we wish to regard u as the independent variable and x as a function of u, we shall prefer to write

$$x = a^u, \quad \text{or} \quad x = \text{antilog } u, \quad \text{or} \quad x = \log^{-1} u.$$

The last form of notation should receive the special attention of the student. The exponent -1 attached to a symbol of *quantity* shows that the quantity is to be used as a *divisor*, instead of a multiplier, in the term into which it enters, e. g., $m^{-1}n = \frac{n}{m}$; or if $n = mx$, $x = m^{-1}n$. See (6). By analogy, then, the exponent -1 is attached to a symbol of *relation* to denote the *inversion* of that relation; so that, for example, if $u = \log x$, $x = \log^{-1} u$.

§ 35. A mathematical **table** is an orderly arrangement of the values of some function for certain selected values of its independent variables. Thus, a table of logarithms contains the logarithms of certain selected numbers (for example, of all integers from 100 to 1000) arranged in the order of magnitude and in a form convenient for reference.

The independent variables, of which the successive values are assumed arbitrarily, and generally at equal intervals, are called the **arguments** of the table. A table of logarithms is a table of *one* argument, namely the antilogarithm; a multiplication table is a table of *two* arguments, namely the two factors. Most of the *Three and Four Place Tables* are tables of one argument, and their argument is generally distinguished by being printed in **full-faced** type.

§ **36.** The **tabulated values** of either the argument or the function in any table are those that are explicitly contained in the table. The difference between two successive tabulated values of either quantity is called a **tabular difference.** The letter $\varDelta$ followed by the letter which denotes any quantity is used by all writers to denote the difference between two values of that quantity. We shall here employ this notation to designate a *tabular* difference. Thus, if x denotes the argument of a table, and u the function, and if two successive tabulated values of x are x_1 and x_2, and the corresponding values of u are u_1 and u_2, then the corresponding tabular differences are

$$\varDelta x = x_2 - x_1, \qquad \varDelta u = u_2 - u_1.$$

The tabular difference of the *argument* generally has a *fixed value* throughout any given table; but this is not always the case.

When a value of any quantity is intermediate between two successive tabulated values, such value may be said to *lie within* the corresponding tabular difference.

§ **37.** A table may be used in two ways: *directly* and *inversely.* The direct use of the table consists in finding the value of the function for an assumed value of the argument; the inverse use, in finding the value of the argument for an assumed value of the function. In either case, if the assumed value is tabulated, the required value is readily found by inspection; but if the assumed value is not tabulated, we must resort to **interpolation.**

§ **38.** We shall not enter on the complete theory of interpolation, but shall confine ourselves to *simple* interpolation, which is all that is necessary in the tables we have to explain. Simple interpolation rests on the principle that **corresponding values of the argument and the function lie within corresponding tabular differences, and divide those differences in the same ratio.** This principle, which is called the principle of **proportional parts**, is applicable, with approximate correctness, to a table of logarithms, provided the tabular differences are made sufficiently small, as we have proved in § 15; and in every properly constructed logarithmic table, the tabular differences are made sufficiently small to permit the application of the principle up to the limit of accuracy belonging to the table.

If, in any mathematical table to which simple interpolation is applicable, x_1 and x_2 are two successive tabulated values of the argument, and u_1 and u_2 the corresponding values of the function, and if x and u are any two corresponding intermediate values of the argument and function, then the principle of proportional parts gives:—

$$\frac{u - u_1}{x - x_1} = \frac{u_2 - u}{x_2 - x} = \frac{u_2 - u_1}{x_2 - x_1} = \frac{\Delta u}{\Delta x}; \qquad (24)$$

whence we derive the following formulas:—

$$u = u_1 + \frac{x - x_1}{\Delta x} \Delta u, \qquad (25)$$

$$u = u_2 - \frac{x_2 - x}{\Delta x} \Delta u, \qquad (26)$$

$$x = x_1 + \frac{u - u_1}{\Delta u} \Delta x, \qquad (27)$$

$$x = x_2 - \frac{u_2 - u}{\Delta u} \Delta x. \qquad (28)$$

If, then, x is given, u may be found by either (25) or (26); and if u is given, x may be found by either (27) or (28).

In these formulas, the first term of the second member may be regarded as an approximate value of the required quantity, and the second term as a **correction** to be applied to that approximate value. The approximate value of the required quantity is that tabulated value which corresponds to *either of the two tabulated values of the assumed quantity between which the given value lies.* Whichever of these two values be taken, the same result will be obtained by the above formulas; but it is best to form the habit of taking that tabulated value which is *nearest* to the given value, whether above it or below it, because that course is preferable in some *abbreviated* methods of interpolation which we shall presently have to explain.

§ 39. If, as it often happens, $\Delta x = 1$, (25–28) become

$$u = u_1 + (x - x_1)\Delta u, \qquad (29)$$

$$u = u_2 - (x_2 - x)\Delta u, \qquad (30)$$

$$x = x_1 + \frac{u - u_1}{\Delta u}, \qquad (31)$$

$$x = x_2 - \frac{u_2 - u}{\Delta u}. \qquad (32)$$

§ 40. The figures of the correction found are generally to be carried out only to a certain numeral place determined by the nature of the table in which the correction is applied. If, in this case, the figures rejected amount to more than half a unit in the place of the last figure retained; that is, to more than five units in the place of the first figure rejected; **the last figure retained is to be increased by 1**; for the figures retained will thus most accurately represent the true value of the correction. For example, 18.723 lies between 18 and 19, but is nearer to the latter than the former, since it exceeds 18.5. Hence if the decimal is rejected, the number should be represented by 19, rather than by 18. On the other hand, 672.18 should be represented by 672, not by 673, if the decimal is rejected.

If that which is rejected is precisely 5 in the first rejected place, it is equally correct to increase the last figure retained and to leave it unchanged. Some computers adopt the rule for this case of increasing the last figure retained if it is odd, and not if it is even, so as to increase it in half the cases that occur in the long run, and to leave it unchanged in the other half. According to this rule, we should convert 3.5, 106.5, 24.5, 11.5 into 4, 106, 24, 12. But sometimes a reason for adopting some different proceeding may suggest itself.

The precepts of this section should be applied to all cases in computation in which the figures of any number are rejected beyond a certain numeral place.

§ 41. We shall illustrate what has been said in the foregoing sections by reference to the following fragment of a four-place table of denary logarithms: —

x	100	101	102	103	104	105	106	107	108	109	x
u	0000	0043	0086	0128	0170	0212	0253	0294	0334	0374	u
Δu		43	43	42	42	42	41	41	40	40	Δu

The argument of this table is the antilogarithm, designated by x, and it is tabulated from 100 to 109, its tabular difference being constant and equal to 1. The function is the mantissa of the logarithm, which is printed without the decimal-point. Its tabular difference varies from 43 to 40 (or, more properly, from .0043 to .0040). The characteristic of a logarithm can readily be found by § **29**; and it is therefore omitted in the modern tables.

The number 108.2 and its logarithm may be said to *lie within* the last tabular differences of this table, according to the phraseology of § **36**.

§ **42.** The following examples of interpolation are adapted to the little table of logarithms given in the last section: —

Ex. 1. Find log 10.537. Here, by § **29**, the characteristic is 1, and we have only to find the mantissa, which by § **27**, is the same as that of 105.37. The nearest tabulated value of the antilogarithm is here 105. We have then

$$x_1 = 105,\ u_1 = 0212,\ \varDelta x = 1,\ \varDelta u = 41,\ x - x_1 = 0.37.$$

The correction to be added to u_1 is then, by (29),

$$0.37 \times 41 = 15.17,$$

of which the unit-figure is to be added to the fourth figure of u_1. The decimal is, then, to be added to *unknown* figures of u_1, and it is, therefore, useless, and should be rejected. We have then

$$\begin{array}{rl} \text{mant log } 105 &= 0212 \\ 0.37 \times 41 &= \underline{\ \ 15} \\ \text{mant log } 10537 &= 0227 \end{array} \therefore \log 10.537 = 1.0227.$$

Ex. 2. Find log 1017.95. Here we adopt 102, rather than 101, as the *nearest* tabulated value; and we have, by (30), since $102 - 101.795 = 0.205$,

$$\begin{array}{rl} \text{mant log } 102 &= 0086 \\ 0.205 \times 43 &= \underline{\ \ \ \ 9} \\ \text{mant log } 101795 &= 0077 \end{array} \therefore \log 1017.95 = 3.0077.$$

Here $0.205 \times 43 = 8.815$, which is represented by 9, according to the precept of § **40**.

COMPUTATION BY LOGARITHMS.

Ex. 3. Find log 0.01068.

mant log 107 = 0294
0.2. × 41 =   8
mant log 1068 = 0286   ∴ log 0.01068 = 8.0286 − 10.

Ex. 4. Find log^{-1} 0.0157. The nearest tabulated mantissa is 0170. Hence we have, by (32),

0170 = mant log 104
$\frac{13}{42}$ =   0.3
0157 = mant log 1037 ∴ log^{-1} 0.0157 = 1.037.

The antilogarithm should generally be computed, as in this instance, to *only one place beyond the tabulated figures.*

Ex. 5. Find log^{-1} (7.0102 − 10).

0086 = mant log 102
$\frac{16}{42}$ =   0.4
0102 = mant log 1024 ∴ log^{-1} (7.0102 − 10) = 0.001024.

§ 43. If we suppose the argument of a table to undergo a gradual and uniform change of value, the function will, at the same time, pass through a gradual, but not generally uniform, change. Thus, if x in the table of § 41 increases at a uniform rate from 100 to 109, log x will increase continuously, though more and more slowly. Now the **derivative** of a function is another function which measures the *rate of change* of the original function as compared with its variable, at the moment that the variable passes through any given value; and this secondary function can always be found by methods of the higher mathematics. In some of the *Three and Four Place Tables*, the value of the derivative is given for each tabulated value of the function, and **can** be used as a *multiplier*, instead of $\frac{\Delta u}{\Delta x}$, in the formulas of interpolation, through *half the tabular difference before and* *after* the tabulated value against which it stands. This depends on the principle already cited in § **38**; for it merely assumes that the function varies at a uniform rate, as compared with the variable, through one tabular difference.

§ **44.** The results obtained by logarithms are liable to errors, which arise from the use of only a certain number of decimal-places of the logarithms. The greater this number of places, the greater will be the degree of accuracy of the results, supposing the data to be accurately known. But it must be remembered that, in any practical computation, the *data themselves* are subject to errors of a certain magnitude, resulting from the imperfection of the means by which they are obtained; and it is a mere waste of labor to employ logarithms which will enable us to carry the results to a greater number of places than the accuracy of the data warrants. "Of the misuse of tables," says De Morgan, " no instance is more common than that which consists in taking tables of too many places of figures." In astronomy and geodesy, the precision of instruments and methods justifies the use of seven-place tables. But in ordinary work, such as that of navigation or common surveying, the accuracy of the results furnished by a four-place table is as great as we need or can expect to attain; and as four-place logarithms take, in the long run, only half the time required by those of five places, and one-fourth of that required by those of seven places, it is desirable to employ them for all purposes which they will serve. A four-place table is also well adapted to be used in instruction, where the leading object is the inculcation of principles. But the student who wishes to become a skilful computer must, after acquiring the command of such a table, familiarize himself with those of five, six, and seven places as well.

Three-place logarithms may be used advantageously

in rapid work preliminary to a detailed computation, and wherever only a low degree of accuracy is required.

§ **45.** Before entering on the explanation of particular tables, we would call the attention of the student to a few general principles of work. First, the beginner in the use of tables should take pains to learn the best methods of dealing with them, the most convenient way of holding them, the simplest order to be followed in consulting them, and the proper employment of the helps to interpolation with which they are provided; and to learn these things he must begin by making a careful study of their plan. Secondly, he must form the habit of using them with strict attention to rule, and especially of interpolating with accuracy, when the best possible results are sought. But, thirdly, it must be remembered that the object of logarithms is to shorten numerical work. This object is only fully accomplished, when the computer can use his table rapidly, and interpolate, both directly and inversely, at a glance. A great deal of this facility can be gained in a short time by practice; and the learner should do his best to acquire it, so far as he can do so without losing his habit of correct work. We may add that the computer ought to keep his eyes open, and avoid falling into mistakes from which a little common sense would be enough to save him.

Among points which belong under the head of accuracy, we would refer again to the precept of § **40**; that, when figures are rejected at the end of a number, amounting to more than half a unit in the place of the last figure retained, *the last figure retained should be increased by* 1. Another rule in which the student requires instruction is that *zeros at the end of a decimal should not be omitted;* for although they do not affect the value of the number, they show that its value is *known to a certain number* *of places*. For a similar reason, when zero is the characteristic of a logarithm, it is always written, and it is a good habit to write it in the case of any decimal number between 0 and 1. Thus, log 1.04, if we are using four-place logarithms, is written 0.0170, not simply .017, for the last form would leave the fourth decimal figure altogether in doubt, and would suggest a question whether the characteristic had been thought of. Lastly, the student must observe that it is as great an offence against the spirit of accuracy to carry out a result beyond the number of places which its logarithm justifies as it is to fall short of that number. Thus, we have found (§ 42, *Ex. 4*), $\log^{-1} 0.0157 = 1.037$. We might carry out the correction of the tabulated number indefinitely, obtaining

$$\tfrac{13}{42} = 0.309524\ldots,$$
$$\log^{-1} 0.0157 = 1.03690476\ldots$$

But this would be to restrict too closely the number determined by a four-place logarithm. In fact, the antilogarithm of 0.0157.. may lie anywhere between

$$1.03669\ldots = \log^{-1} 0.0156500\ldots$$
$$\text{and } 1.03693\ldots = \log^{-1} 0.0157500\ldots$$

If we assume that the value of the given logarithm is $0.0157000\ldots$, its antilogarithm is $1.036812\ldots$ In working with four-place tables, we commonly carry out our antilogarithms to four (or sometimes, in the early part of the table, to five) significant figures; but the last figure must be regarded as *probable*, rather than absolutely certain, owing to the accumulation of small errors in the various logarithms employed to obtain the result. Thus, slightly different answers are sometimes found by different methods of performing one example, or even in looking out a single logarithm or antilogarithm by different processes of interpolation. This ought not to produce any distrust of the method of logarithms, but rather to impress on the student the fact that results derived from imperfect data must be subject to corresponding imperfections. In general, it may be said that, in all computations, whether logarithms are used or not, the results should not be liable to such errors as would be perceptible in observation; nor is it a sound method of working to attempt to carry them decidedly beyond the point of accuracy which observation could detect.

All that has been said in this section must be modified by the remark that the experienced computer may and should permit himself a freedom in the use of his tables which would be unsafe for a beginner. But good habits of approximate work are only acquired by those who have first learned to be exact.

Table of Proportional Parts.

§ 46. This table is designed to be used in connexion with other tables, as an aid in *interpolation*. It contains the product of every integer from 1 to 100 by every *tenth* from 0.1 to 0.9; and is readily used for multiplying any number of two figures by any decimal. The table is arranged in five rows of twenty columns each. The value of the multiplicand is printed in full-faced type over every fifth column, and the values of the multiplier are printed, without the decimal-point, on the right and left of each row of columns. The products are given as if the multipliers were *tenths*. Thus $0.7 \times 28 = 19.6$, and this result is found in the column of 28 and the line of 7. If the multiplier is in the place of *hundredths*, *thousandths*, or any other numeral place, it is only necessary to make a change in the place of the decimal-point in the product. Thus $0.03 \times 62 = 1.86$. To multiply a number of two figures by any decimal, we must find the products which correspond to the successive figures of the multiplier and add them together. The decimal part of the

4

result is generally to be discarded, and in that case the rule of § **40** must be observed. Thus, let it be required to find 0.619×37. We have

$$0.6 \times 37 = 22.2$$
$$0.01 \times 37 = 0.37$$
$$0.009 \times 37 = 0.333$$
$$\therefore 0.619 \times 37 = \overline{23}.$$

In like manner, we find $0.27 \times 15 = 4$, $0.59 \times 73 = 43$, $0.78 \times 69 = 54$, $0.96 \times 84 = 81$, $0.36 \times 57 = 21$, $0.289 \times 51 = 15$, $0.483 \times 93 = 45$, $0.374 \times 82 = 31$.

The table can also be used *inversely*. Thus, let it be required to find, to two places of decimals, what part 36 is of 79. Looking in the column of 79, we find $31.6 = 0.4 \times 79$; $36 - 31.6 = 4.4$, and the tabulated product nearest to this is $4.74 = 0.06 \times 79$.

$$\therefore \tfrac{36}{79} = 0.46.$$

In like manner, we find $\tfrac{29}{68} = 0.43$, $\tfrac{73}{86} = 0.81$, $\tfrac{31}{96} = 0.32$, $\tfrac{27}{74} = 0.37$, $\tfrac{37}{47} = 0.79$, $\tfrac{14}{47} = 0.30$.

The student should practise himself in the use of this table till he can obtain such results as those found in this section mentally and by a rapid glance.

Three-Place Table of Logarithms of Numbers.

§ 47. This table contains, to three places of decimals, the mantissa of the denary logarithm of every number of *one* or *two* significant figures. The antilogarithm is the argument of the table, and is printed in full-faced type, the first significant figure being given in the left-hand column, and the second significant figure (for which **0** is to be substituted, if there is but one significant figure) at the top of the table. The mantissa of the logarithm is given, in common type, in the line and column determined by the two figures of the antilogarithm. Thus,

COMPUTATION BY LOGARITHMS.   39

we find log 8.7 = 0.940, log 7 = 0.845, log 0.61 = 9.785 — 10.

The last line of the table contains the logarithms of numbers of three figures, beginning with 10. Thus, we find log 1070 = 3.029.

The three-place logarithm of any number whatever and the antilogarithm of any three-place logarithm can be found from this table by the method explained and exemplified in §§ 38–42, and the process may be shortened by the use of the table of Proportional Parts. The antilogarithm should be computed *to one figure only beyond those tabulated*, as it cannot be determined more accurately by its three-place logarithm. It must be observed that, in their order of succession, the logarithms run across each line from left to right, and then begin again at the left of the next line.

Let the student find the following logarithms and antilogarithms by this table : —

log 437.2   = 2.640,   log 0.694   = 9.841 — 10,
log   2.78 = 0.444,   log 17.92   = 1.253,
log 32910. = 4.518,   log 0.00217 = 7.336 — 10;

$\log^{-1}$ 2.335 = 216, $\log^{-1}$ 0.794 = 6.23,
$\log^{-1}$ 1.872 = 74.5, $\log^{-1}$ (9.647 — 10) = 0.444,
$\log^{-1}$ (8.427 — 10) = 0.0268, $\log^{-1}$ 2.533 = 342.

Four-Place Table of Logarithms of Numbers.

§ 48. The arrangement of this table is similar to that of the three-place table. The antilogarithm is the argument, and is given to *three* significant figures, for the last one or two of which 0 is to be substituted in the case of a number of less than three figures. The first two significant figures must be sought at the left of the table, in the column headed "Natural Numbers," and the third at the top of the table. The *second, third,* and *fourth* decimal-figures of the logarithm will be found in the line and column thus determined, and the *first* decimal-figure in the 0 column, and either on the same line with the first two significant figures of the antilogarithm, or, if no figure stands there in the first decimal place, then on the nearest line above which contains a figure in that place. Thus, log $3.23 = 0.5092$, log $48.6 = 1.6866$, log $7480 = 3.8739$, log $0.285 = 9.4548 - 10$, log $921 = 2.9643$, log $0.0052 = 7.7160 - 10$.

If the second decimal-figure is printed in **small type**, the first decimal-figure is to be sought at the beginning of the **next following line**. Thus, log $2.59 = 0.4133$, log $126 = 2.1004$, log $0.0797 = 8.9015 - 10$, log $63.2 = 1.8007$, log $50400 = 4.7024$.

As in the three-place table, the order of succession of the logarithms is from left to right through the successive lines; but there are no repetitions in this table, and the last logarithm in each line is followed by the first in the next line.

The four-place logarithm of any number or the antilogarithm of any four-place logarithm can be found from this table by the method of §§ **38-42**, by the aid of the table of Proportional Parts, already explained. The antilogarithm should generally be computed to *four figures only*, that is, to one figure beyond the tabulated figures; but in the early part of the table it may be computed to *five* figures. Thus, we have

log $59.43 = 1.7740$, log $0.008147 = 7.9110 - 10$,
log $284.8 = 2.4545$, log $572610. = 5.7579$,
log $0.073748 = 8.8678 - 10$, log $0.5017 = 9.7004 - 10$,
log $3.1607 = 0.4998$, log $99.968 = 1.9999$;

$\log^{-1} 1.9155 = 82.32$, $\log^{-1} (5.8760 - 10) = 0.00007517$,
$\log^{-1} 0.0547 = 1.1342$, $\log^{-1} (8.1577 - 10) = 0.014377$,
$\log^{-1} 3.8291 = 6747$, $\log^{-1} (9.5757 - 10) = 0.3765$.

§ 49. Interpolation in this table is facilitated by the use of the right-hand division of the table, headed "Proportional Parts." If we follow out the line which contains the tabulated logarithm corresponding to the first three significant figures of the given number, we shall find, under the *fourth* significant figure, the correction which corresponds to that figure, pointed off as if the mantissas in the table were whole numbers, and, in like manner, under the *fifth* significant figure of the antilogarithm, we shall find the correction for that figure, provided we move the point in that correction one place to the left, and so on. Thus, suppose it is required to find log 1273.64. We find

mant log. 127 = 1038, correction for .3 = 10.4
     „   „ .06 = 2.09
     „   „ .004 = 0.139
     „   „ .364 = 13

∴ log 1273.64 = 3.1051.

In like manner, we find

log 0.073748 = 8.8678 − 10, log 0.287428 = 9.4586 − 10,
log 3.1607 = 0.4998,   log 10.0086 = 1.0004,
log 908.4   = 2.9583,   log 0.09994 = 8.9998 − 10.

In using this table of Proportional Parts, we should work from the *nearest* tabulated value. For each line of corrections is computed from the *average value* of the tabular difference for that line, and the smaller the proportional part taken, the less is the probability of error. Hence, if the fourth significant figure is as great as 5, we should increase the third significant figure by 1, and from the tabulated logarithm thus obtained *subtract* a suitable correction. For example, suppose it is required to find log 1.2084. We have 120.84 = 121 − 0.16. ˙ Then

mant log 121 = 0828, correction for 0.1 = 3.5
,, ,, 0.06 = 2.09
,, ,, 0.16 = $\overline{6}$
∴ log 1.2084 = 0.0822

In like manner, we find.

log 0.3077 = 9.4882 − 10, log 63.071 = 1.7998,
log 5518.3 = 3.7418,   log 9.426 = 0.9743.

§ 50. This sub-table of Proportional Parts can also be used inversely. Thus, suppose it is required to find $\log^{-1}$ 1.9155. We have

9154 = mant log 823, 9155 = 9154 + 1,
1.1 = correction for 0.2;
∴ $\log^{-1}$ 1.9155 = 82.32.

Again, if $\log^{-1}$ 3.8291 is required, we have

8293 = mant log 675, 8291 = 8293 − 2,
1.9 = correction for 0.3, 675 − 0.3 = 674.7
∴ $\log^{-1}$ 3.8291 = 6747.

In like manner, we find

$\log^{-1}$ 0.4438 = 2.779, $\log^{-1}$ (5.8760 − 10) = 0.00007516,
$\log^{-1}$ 0.0547 = 1.1342, $\log^{-1}$ (8.1577 − 10) = 0.014377,
$\log^{-1}$ 2.8272 = 671.7, $\log^{-1}$ (9.5757 − 10) = 0.3764.

§ 51. The extreme left-hand column of the table of logarithms, headed "Angles," is introduced to facilitate finding the logarithm of the number of minutes in an angle expressed in degrees and minutes or hours and minutes, or of seconds in an angle expressed in minutes and seconds. The unit-figure is to be taken at the top of the table, and the characteristic is always 2. Thus we obtain log (6° 27′) = 2.5877, log (10^h 12^m) = 2.7868, log (4′ 08″) = 2.3945, log (13° 15′.8) = 2.9008.

The small table under the table of logarithms is to be

used for trigonometric work, and will be explained in another place.

Arithmetical Complement. Reciprocal.

§ 52. The **arithmetical complement** of the logarithm of a number, which may also be called the **cologarithm** of the number, is the remainder obtained by subtracting that logarithm from 10. It is commonly denoted by "arco log" or by "colog." The above definition is then expressed by the formula,

$$\operatorname{colog} x = 10 - \log x. \qquad (33)$$

Since

$$10 = 9.99\ldots\ldots 9 + (1 \text{ in the last place}),$$

the arithmetical complement may be found by subtracting each figure of the logarithm from 9, and then, adding 1 to the last figure of the remainder, or, in other words, *by beginning with the characteristic and subtracting each successive figure of the logarithm from 9, down to the last significant figure, and subtracting that figure from 10.* By this method the cologarithm of a number can be written down from inspection of the table almost as rapidly as the logarithm itself. Thus we have

colog 59.43	= 8.2260,	colog 0.008147	= 12.0890,
colog 284.8	= 7.5455,	colog 572610.	= 4.2421,
colog 0.073748	= 11.1322,	colog 0.5017	= 10.2996,
colog 3.1607	= 9.5002,	colog 99.968	= 8 0001,
colog 1273.64	= 6.8949,	colog 908.4	= 7.0417,
colog 0.287428	= 10.5414,	colog 10.0086	= 8.9996,
colog 1.2084	= 9.9178,	colog 0.3077	= 10.5118.

§ 53. By (33) and (9),

$$\operatorname{colog} x - 10 = -\log x = \log \tfrac{1}{x}; \qquad (34)$$

44 THE ELEMENTS OF LOGARITHMS.

that is, *if* 10 *be subtracted from the cologarithm of any number, the remainder is the logarithm of the reciprocal of that number.* Thus we have

$$\dot{5}9.\dot{4}3 = 0.01683, \qquad 0.00\dot{8}14\dot{7} = 122.74,$$
$$2\dot{8}\dot{4}.8 = 0.003512, \qquad 572\dot{6}1\dot{0} = 0.000001746,$$
$$0.07\dot{3}74\dot{8} = 13.560, \qquad 0.\dot{5}1\dot{7} = 1.993,$$
$$3.1\dot{8}07 = 0.3164, \qquad 9\dot{9}.9\dot{8}3 = 0.010002,$$
$$12\dot{7}3.\dot{5}4 = 0.0007850, \qquad \dot{9}08.\dot{4} = 0.0011008,$$
$$0.28\dot{7}42\dot{8} = 3.478, \qquad 10.\dot{0}08\dot{6} = 0.09990,$$
$$1.2\dot{0}8\dot{4} = 0.8276, \qquad 0.3\dot{0}77 = 3.249.$$

Multiplication by Logarithms.

§ 54. Multiplication, division, involution, and evolution are easily performed by logarithms by the aid of the theorems of § **16**. The theorem for multiplication is that *the logarithm of the continued product of several quantities is the sum of their logarithms;* or

$$\log \Pi x = \Sigma \log x.$$

If any of the factors are *less than* 1, their logarithms should be increased by 10, as in § **30**, and *the resulting logarithm diminished by* 10 *times the number of such factors*.

If any of the factors are *negative*, their logarithms are to be taken *without regard to their signs*, and the sign of the result determined by *the rules of algebra*. It is well to write the letter *n* after any logarithm which corresponds to a negative number. Then if the number of logarithms so marked is *odd*, the product is *negative;* if *even*, the product is *positive*. This indicates the usual method of dealing with negative numbers in logarithmic computation.

Ex. 1. Find $908.4 \times (-0.79) \times (-101.92) \times 3.1607 \times (-0.0004)$.

	908.4	log	2.9583
	— 0.79	log	9.8976n — 10
	— 101.92	log	2.0083n
	3.1607	log	0.4998
	— 0.0004	log	6.6021n — 10
Ans.	— 92.50	log	1.9661n

Ex. 2. Find $0.05392 \times 0.9 \times 1534.1 \times 2.117$.

Ans. 157.6.

Ex. 3. Find $(-7.1309) \times 0.004006 \times 0.7172 \times (-0.015) \times 21.362$.   *Ans.* 0.006564.

Division by Logarithms.

§ 55. *The logarithm of a quotient is found by subtracting the logarithm of the divisor from that of the dividend.* By this principle and by (34),

$$\log \frac{x}{y} = \log x - \log y = \log x + \operatorname{colog} y - 10. \quad (35)$$

Hence *the logarithm of a quotient may be found by adding together the logarithm of the dividend and the cologarithm of the divisor and subtracting* 10 *from the result.* The student should habituate himself to working by this latter rule, as it is more convenient than the former, especially where compound operations are to be performed, as in §§ **56** and **59**.

If the characteristic of the dividend is increased by 10, that of the quotient must be diminished by 20.

Ex. 1. Divide 0.9316 by 15.42.

	0.9316	log	9.9692 — 10
	15.42	colog	8.8119
Ans.	0.06041	log	8.7811 — 10

Ex. 2. Divide 0.039008 by — 0.0097.   *Ans.* — 4.022.

Ex. 3. Divide — 67.18 by — 0.4573.   *Ans.* 146.93.

The Rule of Three by Logarithms.

§ 56. If any three terms of a proportion are known, the fourth can be found by the Rule of Three; and the operations required by this rule may be performed, in a single process, by logarithms. See § 17.

Ex. 1. $0.5334 : x = -0.001907 : -2.008$. Find x.

The Rule of Three gives $x = \dfrac{0.5334 \times (-2.008)}{-0.001907}$.

0.5334	log	$9.7270 - 10$
-2.008	log	$0.3028n$
-0.001907	colog	$12.7197n$
$x = 561.7$	log	2.7495

Ex. 2. $-37.82 : 503.7 = 0.09852 : x$. Find x.
Ans. $x = -1.3119$.

Ex. 3. $0.71972 : 3.156 = x : 0.04983$. Find x.
Ans. $x = 0.011363$.

Involution by Logarithms.

§ 57. *The logarithm of any power of a quantity is found by multiplying the logarithm of the quantity by the exponent of the power;* or

$$\log x^n = n \log x.$$

If the logarithm of the given quantity is increased by 10, the product must be diminished by 10 *times the exponent of the required power*, since

$$n (\log x + 10) = n \log x + 10n.$$

The results found by this method are hardly to be relied on beyond the *third* significant figure, since the error in the logarithm of the given quantity is multiplied by the exponent.

Ex. 1. Find the cube of 0.8724.

  0.8724 log 9.9407 — 10
              3
Ans. 0.664 log $\overline{9.8221}$ — 10

Ex. 2. Find the 7th power of 3.051. *Ans.* 2460.

Ex. 3. Find the square of 21.27. *Ans.* 452.5.

Evolution by Logarithms.

§ 58. *The logarithm of any root of a quantity is found by dividing the logarithm of the quantity by the exponent of the root;* or

$$\log \sqrt[n]{x} = \frac{1}{n} \log x.$$

If the characteristic of the logarithm of the given quantity is negative, *it should be increased* before division, not by 10, but *by 10 times the exponent of the required root*, and then the characteristic of the quotient should be *decreased by* 10; for

$$\frac{\log x + 10n}{n} = \frac{\log x}{n} + 10 = \log \sqrt[n]{x} + 10.$$

Ex. 1. Find the 4th root of 0.005627.

    0.005627   4)37.7503 — 40
Ans. 0.2739   log $\overline{9.4376}$ — 10

Ex. 2. Find the 9th root of 0.0007808.

              Ans. 0.4516.

Ex. 3. Find the 5th root of 370.42.

              Ans. 3.264.

Ex. 4. Find the cube of the 11th root of 61.98.

              Ans. 3.081.

Ex. 5. Find the 10th power of the 7th root of 0.8213.

              Ans. 0.7550.

Compound Operations.

§ 59. Examples involving the combination of multiplications, divisions, involutions, and evolutions are especially suited to be solved by logarithms.

Let the student work out the following results:—

Ex. 1.

$$\sqrt[3]{\frac{0.05639 \times 1.0728^3 \times \sqrt[5]{421.3} \times 10.00}{\sqrt[7]{0.007623^{10}} \times 52.46 \times 0.7000}} = 4.068.$$

Ex. 2.

$$\left(\frac{\sqrt[3]{7394.} \times 0.02998}{1.0063^2 \times 57.00}\right)^2 \times \sqrt[5]{\frac{532.4 \times 0.2900}{\sqrt{0.0695} \times 9.995}} = 0.0002309.$$

Ex. 3.

$$\sqrt[3]{\left(\frac{\sqrt[5]{0.01907^3} \times 3.796}{0.05545^2 \times 1000.0 \times 0.0007241}\right)^4} = 857.4.$$

Ex. 4.

$$\sqrt[4]{\frac{\sqrt[3]{43.04} \times 809.8 \times 0.2516^3 \times 0.09093}{2139. \times 3.007 \times \sqrt[11]{0.008188} \times 0.7433^4}} = 0.2386.$$

Ex. 5.

$$\sqrt[5]{\frac{1.0007^5 \times 0.3710}{\sqrt{0.005278}}} \div \frac{\sqrt[3]{45.56} \times 0.2203}{7.197 \times 0.6411} = 8.140.$$

Ex. 6.

$$\left(\frac{0.7628 \times 79328. \times 0.01333^2}{40.07 \times \sqrt[7]{15.21}}\right)^{\frac{100}{187}} = 0.2034.$$

Exponential Equations.

[**§ 60.** We have seen, in § 18, that if $b^x = m$,

$$x = \frac{\log m}{\log b},$$

or log $x = $ log log $m - $ log log b
$\qquad = $ log log $m + $ colog log $b - 10.$ } (36)

Ex. 1. $21^x = 15.75.$ Find x.

$m = 15.75 \quad$ log $1.1973 \quad$ log 0.0783
$b \; = 21 \qquad$ log $1.3222 \quad$ colog $\overline{9.8787}$
$x \; = 0.9058 \qquad\qquad\qquad$ log $\overline{9.9570} - 10$

Ex. 2. $40.56^x = 8276.$ $\;x = 2.437.$]

[§ **61.** If either b or m is less than 1, log b or log m is negative, and we proceed as in § **54.**

Ex. 1. Find x from the equation $0.5175^x = 6.208$.

$m = 6.208 \quad$ log $\;\;0.7930 \qquad\qquad$ log $\;\;9.8993 - 10$
$b \; = 0.5175 \;$ log $\overline{1.7139} = -\, 0.2861 \;$ colog $\;\underline{10.5434n}$
$x \; = -\, 2.771. \qquad\qquad\qquad$ log $\;\;0.4427n$

Ex. 2. Find x from the equation $0.027907^x = 0.8213$.
$\qquad\qquad\qquad\qquad\qquad\qquad$ *Ans.* $x = 0.05501$.]

[§ **62.** It has already been remarked in § 19 that solving an exponential equation by logarithms is equivalent to *converting a logarithm from one system to another.* Thus, in the above examples, we have found the following logarithms from their values in the denary system: —

$\log_{21} \;\; 15.75 = 0.9058, \;\; \log_{0.5175} \; 6.208 = -\, 2.771,$
$\log_{40.56} \; 8276 = 2.437, \;\; \log_{0.027907} \; 0.8213 = 0.05501.]$

Logarithms of Sums and Differences.

[§ **63.** Addition and Subtraction cannot be performed by logarithms. Hence arise inconvenience and liability to error, when these operations occur in the midst of others which can be performed by logarithms. The table of *Logarithms of Sums and Differences* is one form of a table proposed by Gauss to obviate this difficulty.

The *argument* of this table, designated by the letter A, is any logarithm, which we may call log x. Its characteristic (increased by 10, if negative) is at the top of the table, and the first two figures of the mantissa are in the left-hand column. The remaining figures of the mantissa are 0 for the tabulated values of the argument. The *function* given in the table, designated by B, is log $(x + 1)$. Its characteristic, accompanied sometimes by one or two figures of the mantissa, is printed at the top and bottom of each column. The remaining figures are to be found in the body of the table; the first of them being printed only in the first line in which it has a new value and also in the first line of each division of five lines. When this first figure is in *small type*, the earlier figures of B are to be taken from the *foot* of the column; otherwise they are to be taken from the top of the column.

We shall call B, or log $(x + 1)$, the *Gaussian* of A, or log x, and A the *anti-Gaussian* of B; and we shall use the symbols $\mathfrak{G}$ and $\mathfrak{G}^{-1}$ to designate these relations. Thus we write

$$B = \mathfrak{G}A, \text{ or } \log(x+1) = \mathfrak{G} \log x,$$
$$A = \mathfrak{G}^{-1}B, \text{ or } \log(x-1) = \mathfrak{G}^{-1} \log x; \quad (37)$$

where the exponent -1 is used according to the principle laid down in § **34**.

We have then

$\mathfrak{G}\,(9.2100 - 10) = 0.0653, \quad \mathfrak{G}\,\,0.9800 = 1.0232,$
$\mathfrak{G}\,\,0.6300 = 0.7215, \quad \mathfrak{G}\,(8.4800 - 10) = 0.0129.$

These results may be verified by means of the table of Logarithms of Numbers; which gives, for instance,

$\log^{-1}(9.2100 - 10) = 0.1622 = x,$
$\log(x + 1) = \log 1.1622 = 0.0653.$]

[§ **64.** The Gaussian or anti-Gaussian of any four-place

logarithm may be found to four decimal-places from this table by simple interpolation. In the principal columns of the table, a *multiplier* (derivative), to be used instead of the tabular difference, is printed in small type after each value of the function. This multiplier should properly be used *through half the tabular interval on each side* of the value to which it is attached; or, in other words, we should apply our correction to the *nearest* tabulated value. The general table of Proportional Parts may be used in computing corrections.

The multiplier is omitted in the earlier columns of the table, where the tabular differences are so small that corrections are easily computed, and also in the later columns, after the occurrence of the letter c, where its value is 100, and A and B vary by equal amounts.

The table extends only from $A = 6.0000 - 10$ to $A = 4.0000$. The reason of this limitation is that

if $A < 6.0000 - 10$, $B = 0.0000$ to four places,
and if $A > 4.0000$, $B = A$ to four places.

Let the student find the following values from this table: —

ⓑ 1.0960   = 1.1295,   ⓑ 3.8129   = 3.8130,
ⓑ (7.5265 − 10) = 0.0015,   ⓑ (9.6431 − 10) = 0.1582.

ⓑ⁻¹1.0960 = 1.0597,   ⓑ⁻¹3.8129 = 3.8128,
ⓑ⁻¹0.1051 = 9.4373 − 10,   ⓑ⁻¹1.0216 = 0.9782.]

[§ **65.** If m and n are any two numbers, we have

$$m + n = n\left(\frac{m}{n} + 1\right), \quad m - n = n\left(\frac{m}{n} - 1\right),$$

$$\log(m+n) = \log n + \log\left(\frac{m}{n} + 1\right),$$

$$\log(m-n) = \log n + \log\left(\frac{m}{n} - 1\right);$$

or, by (37),

$$\left.\begin{aligned}\log(m+n) &= \log n + \mathfrak{G}\log\frac{m}{n} \\ &= \log n + \mathfrak{G}(\log m + \operatorname{colog} n), \\ \log(m-n) &= \log n + \mathfrak{G}^{-1}\log\frac{m}{n} \\ &= \log n + \mathfrak{G}^{-1}(\log m + \operatorname{colog} n);\end{aligned}\right\} \quad (38)$$

and by these formulas we can obtain $\log(m+n)$ and $\log(m-n)$ when $\log m$ and $\log n$ are known, without having to find m and n themselves.

Putting in (38) $m=1$ and $n=x$, we have, by (7),

$$\left.\begin{aligned}\log(1+x) &= \log x + \mathfrak{G}\operatorname{colog} x, \\ \log(1-x) &= \log x + \mathfrak{G}^{-1}(\operatorname{colog} x)\end{aligned}\right\} \quad (39)$$

Formulas (37–39) will be found at the bottom of the table.]

[§ **66.** The use of this table is illustrated by the following examples: —

Ex. 1. Find the hypotenuse h of a right triangle of which the legs are $a=43.76$ and $b=71.02$.

The Pythagorean Proposition gives $h^2 = a^2+b^2$, or, $h=\sqrt{(a^2+b^2)}$. Working without the Gaussian table, we have

$$\begin{array}{llll} a=43.76 & \log 1.6411 & b=71.02 & \log 1.8514 \\ & 2 & & 2 \\ a^2=1915 & \log 3.2822 & & \log 3.7028 \\ b^2=5044 \\ a^2+b^2=6959 & 2)3.8425 \\ h=83.40 & \log 1.9212 \end{array}$$

The Gaussian method saves two references to the table. By that method we have

COMPUTATION BY LOGARITHMS.   53

$\log a = 1.6411$
$\operatorname{colog} b = 8.1486$

$\log \dfrac{a}{b} = 9.7897 - 10$

$\log \dfrac{a^2}{b^2} = 9.5794 - 10$ ⑤ $0.1397 = \log \dfrac{a^2 + b^2}{b^2}$

$\tfrac{1}{2}$ ⑤ $0.0698 = \log \dfrac{\sqrt{a^2 + b^2}}{b}$

$\log b\ \underline{1.8514}$

$h = 83.40 \qquad \log\ \ 1.9212$

Ex. 2. Compute

$$\dfrac{(0.2194)^2 \times \sqrt[3]{915.7} + 4.4 \times \sqrt[5]{0.7 \times 32.03}}{(571.6 \times 0.0235 - 0.04004 \times 6.72 \times 10.97)^3}.$$

Ans. 0.1143.]

APPENDIX.

EXPLANATION OF THE TRIGONOMETRIC TABLES.

(§ **1.**) The following formulas, in which φ denotes any angle, are proved in Trigonometry:—

$$\left.\begin{array}{l} \log \sin \varphi = \operatorname{colog} \csc \varphi - 10, \\ \log \csc \varphi = \operatorname{colog} \sin \varphi - 10, \\ \log \tan \varphi = \operatorname{colog} \operatorname{ctn} \varphi - 10, \\ \log \operatorname{ctn} \varphi = \operatorname{colog} \tan \varphi - 10, \\ \log \sec \varphi = \operatorname{colog} \cos \varphi - 10, \\ \log \cos \varphi = \operatorname{colog} \sec \varphi - 10. \end{array}\right\} \text{(A)}$$

See Seaver's Formulas, **6**; Peirce's Trigonometry, § 10; Chauvenet's Trigonometry, § 19; Elements of Logarithms, § 53.

$$\left.\begin{array}{l} \sin (90° - \varphi) = \cos \varphi, \\ \csc (90° - \varphi) = \sec \varphi, \\ \tan (90° - \varphi) = \operatorname{ctn} \varphi, \\ \operatorname{ctn} (90° - \varphi) = \tan \varphi, \\ \sec (90° - \varphi) = \csc \varphi, \\ \cos (90° - \varphi) = \sin \varphi. \end{array}\right\} \text{(B)}$$

See Seaver, **35**; Peirce, § 7; Chauvenet, §§ 18, 38.

$$\left.\begin{array}{rl}
\sin(90°+\varphi) &= \cos\varphi, \\
\cos(90°+\varphi) &= -\sin\varphi, \\
\tan(90°+\varphi) &= -\ctn\varphi; \\
\sin\varphi = & (-)^k \sin(2k\,90°+\varphi) \\
= & -(-)^k \cos([2k+1]\,90°+\varphi), \\
\cos\varphi = & (-)^k \cos(2k\,90°+\varphi) \\
= & (-)^k \sin([2k+1]\,90°+\varphi), \\
\tan\varphi = & \tan(2k\,90°+\varphi) \\
= & -\ctn([2k+1]\,90°+\varphi).
\end{array}\right\} \quad (C)$$

See Seaver, **35, 28, 29, 30**; Peirce, §§ 63, 65, 68; Chauvenet, §§ 38, 41, 43, 45, 51, 52.

$$\left.\begin{array}{c|cccc}
 & \text{1st Qu.} & \text{2nd Qu.} & \text{3rd Qu.} & \text{4th Qu.} \\
\sin & + & + & - & - \\
\cos & + & - & - & + \\
\tan & + & - & + & -
\end{array}\right\} \quad (D)$$

See Seaver, **4, 5**; Peirce, §§ 62, 66; Chauvenet, § 47.

Three-Place Table of Trigonometric Functions.

(**§ 2.**) This table contains the values of the six simple trigonometric functions, generally to three significant figures, and their logarithms to three places of decimals, for every degree of the quadrant. The logarithms of the functions occupy the left-hand division of the table, and the natural values the right-hand division. The degrees run down the left-hand column of the table to 45°, and then up the right-hand column. The names of the functions are to be taken from the *top* of the page when the degrees are taken from the *left-hand* column, marked ° at the top, and from the *bottom* of the page when the degrees are taken from the *right-hand* column marked ° at the bottom. The integral part of the value of the function, whether natural or logarithmic, is generally printed only at the top and bottom of the column, unless it changes its value in the column. *The characteristics, when negative, are increased by* 10, *so as to become positive.* This is the case with the log sin and log cos of all angles and with the log tan of angles less than 45° and the log ctn of angles greater than 45°. We shall find it convenient to follow this usage in citing the logarithmic functions, in our illustrations, and to leave the term — 10 to be added (or remembered) by the student when he employs the functions in examples. We have then

sin 17° = 0.292,   tan 17° = 0.306,   sec 17° = 1.046,
csc 17° = 3.42   ctn 17° = 3.27,   cos 17° = 0.956;

log sin 17° = 9.466, log tan 17° = 9.485, log sec 17° = 0.019,
log csc 17° = 0.534, log ctn 17° = 0.515, log cos 17° = 9.981;

sin 52° = 0.788,   tan 52° = 1.28,   sec 52° = 1.62,
csc 52° = 1.269,   ctn 52° = 0.781,   cos 52° = 0.616;

log sin 52° = 9.897, log tan 52° = 0.107, log sec 52° = 0.211,
log csc 52° = 0.103, log ctn 52° = 9.893, log cos 52° = 9.789.

The method of **simple interpolation** explained in the treatise on Logarithms, §§ **38–42**, may be applied to this table both directly and inversely. The tabular differences are printed between the lines in small type, except for the last two columns of logarithmic functions. The table of Proportional Parts may be used in computing the corrections. The student must be careful to observe whether the correction, in any given case, should be applied to the tabulated value by *addition* or *subtraction*. This can be determined by the theorem that the *sine*, *tangent*, and *secant* of an acute angle *increase* with the increase of the angle, while the *cosine*, *cotangent*, and *cosecant decrease;* or, more simply, by the principle that *corresponding values of the argument and the function must lie within corresponding tabular differences.* For example, to find the functions of 71°.8, we apply to those of 72° *two-tenths,* or to those of 71° *eight-tenths,* of the tabular differences for the interval between 71° and 72°, adding or subtracting in each case so as to bring the result *between the tabulated values for* 71° *and* 72°. Thus we obtain

$$\sin 71°.8 = 0.946 + 0.004 = 0.951 - 0.001 = 0.950,$$
$$\csc 71°.8 = 1.058 - 0.006 = 1.051 + 0.001 = 1.052,$$
$$\tan 71°.8 = 2.90 + 0.14 = 3.08 - 0.04 = 3.04,$$
$$\ctn 71°.8 = 0.344 - 0.015 = 0.325 + 0.004 = 0.329,$$
$$\sec 71°.8 = 3.07 + 0.14 = 3.24 - 0.03 = 3.21,$$
$$\cos 71°.8 = 0.326 - 0.014 = 0.309 + 0.003 = 0.312;$$
$$\log \sin 71°.8 = 9.976 + 0.002 = 9.978 - 0.000 = 9.978,$$
$$\log \csc 71°.8 = 0.024 - 0.002 = 0.022 + 0.000 = 0.022,$$
$$\log \tan 71°.8 = 0.463 + 0.020 = 0.488 - 0.005 = 0.483,$$
$$\log \ctn 71°.8 = 9.537 - 0.020 = 9.512 + 0.005 = 9.517,$$
$$\log \sec 71°.8 = 0.487 + 0.018 = 0.510 - 0.005 = 0.505,$$
$$\log \cos 71°.8 = 9.513 - 0.018 = 9.490 + 0.005 = 9.495.$$

The two methods of interpolation here indicated lead to the same result. But the best habit, as we have remarked in the book on Logarithms, is that of working from the *nearest* tabulated value, which is, in this case, 72°.

In the **inverse** use of this table, where an angle is found from the logarithm of one of its trigonometric functions, the result should be expressed to *the nearest tenth of a degree*. E.g., if

$$\log \tan \varphi = 0.367,$$

the nearest tabulated value of the log tan is $0.372 = \log \tan 67°$; then, using formula (32) of the book on Logarithms, we have

$$\Delta u = 21, \ u_2 - u = 5, \ \frac{u_2 - u}{\Delta u} = \tfrac{5}{21} = 0.2,$$
$$\varphi = 67° - 0.2 = 66°.8.$$

In like manner, let the student find the following values: —

If $\log \sin \varphi = 9.325$, $\varphi = 12°.2$; if $\cos \varphi = 0.494$, $\varphi = 60°.4$, if $\log \ctn \varphi = 9.960$, $\varphi = 47°.6$; if $\ctn \varphi = 2.65$, $\varphi = 20°.7$.

APPENDIX. 59

(§ **3.**) It is to be observed that the *two angles*, taken from *opposite sides* of the page, which correspond to any one number, found or interpolated in a given column of the table, are *complements* of each other, and also that the *two names* of any column, given at the *top and bottom* of the page, and corresponding to the two angles, are *complementary*. Thus,

$0.292 = \sin 17° = \cos 73°$, $\quad 0.494 = \cos 60°.4 = \sin 29°.6$,
$0.107 = \log \tan 52°$ $\qquad 9.633 = \log \tan 23°.2$
$\quad\; = \log \ctn 38°$, $\qquad\quad\; = \log \ctn 66°.8$.

This relation is in accordance with formula (B) of (§ 1).*

Again, it will be seen that the log sin and log csc, the log tan and log ctn, the log sec and log cos are respectively *arithmetical complements*. Thus,

log tan 17° $= 9.485$, log ctn 17° $= 0.515 =$ co 9.485;
log sec 52° $= 0.211$, log cos 52° $= 9.789 =$ co 0.211;
log sin 71°.8 $= 9.978$, log csc 71°.8 $= 0.022 =$ co 9.978.

This relation agrees with (§ 1) (A), since 10 should be subtracted from one of the logarithms of each pair, as taken from the table, in order to reduce it to true value. It is a consequence of this relation that the *tabular differences* are alike in the columns of log sin and log csc, also in the columns of log tan and log ctn, and lastly in the columns of log sec and log cos. The pairs of columns thus related are bracketed together in the logarithmic part of the table, so that the six columns are printed as three double columns.

Other formulas of trigonometry, such as

$$\log \tan \varphi = \log \sin \varphi + \log \sec \varphi,$$
$$\log \cos \varphi = \log \sin \varphi + \log \ctn \varphi,$$
$$\sin^2 \varphi + \cos^2 \varphi = 1, \; \sec^2 \varphi - \tan^2 \varphi = 1, \; \&c.,$$

---

* The numbers of the sections of the Appendix are distinguished from those of the book by being included in *parentheses*.

are readily verified by this table. Thus we have

$$\log \sin 78° = 9.990$$
$$\underline{\log \sec 78° = 0.682}$$
$$\log \sin 78° + \log \sec 78° = 0.672$$
$$\log \tan 78° = 0.673;$$

where a slight discrepancy arises from the accumulation of errors in the addition of the logarithms.

Again,

$$\log \tan 22° = 9.606$$
$$\log \tan^2 22° = 9.212$$
$$(\S 3) \log \tan^2 22° = \log (1 + \tan^2 22°) = 0.066$$
$$\therefore \log \sec 22° = \tfrac{1}{2} \log (1 + \tan^2 22°) = 0.033.$$

(§ 4.) Where the printed tabular differences are omitted near the top of a column, being printed in the lower part of the same column, the principle of interpolation cannot properly be applied to the table. In this case, we may employ the **small table** in the upper right-hand corner of the page. The *direct use* of this table is to find the log sin or log tan of a small angle, by finding the logarithm of the angle itself, expressed in degrees, and adding to that logarithm a logarithm (S for the log sin or T for the log tan) of which the value is given in the small table. Thus, we have

$$\log \sin 5°.23 = 0.718 + 8.241 = 8.959,$$
$$\log \tan 5°.23 = 0.718 + 8.243 = 8.961.$$

The log csc and log ctn, as we have seen in (§ 3), are the arithmetical complements of the log sin and log tan. E.g.,

$$\log \csc 5°.23 = 1.041, \log \ctn 5°.23 = 1.039.$$

The natural csc and ctn are the *antilogarithms* of the log csc and log ctn. E.g.,

$$\csc 5°.23 = 11.00, \ctn 5°.23 = 10.95.$$

APPENDIX.

The log cos, log ctn, log sec, log tan, and natural sec and tan of an angle near 90° are, by (B), found by finding the *complementary* functions of the *complement* of that angle. E.g.,

log cos 83°.81 = log sin 6°.19 = 0.791 + 8.241 = 9.032,
log ctn 83°.81 = 9.035,   log sec 83°.81 = 0.968,
   log tan 83°.81 = 0.965,
sec 83°.81 = 9.30,   tan 83°.81 = 9.22.

This table can also be used *inversely*. Thus, to find the angle whose log sin is 9.123. The large table shows that it is between 7° and 8°. $\therefore S = 8.241$ or 8.240. 9.123 − 8.240 = 0.883 = log (7.64 < 7.83). $\therefore S = 8.241$. 9.123 − 8.241 = 0.882 = log 7.62, $\therefore$ 9.123 = log sin 7°.62.

In like manner, we find

9.055 = log sin 6°.51,   9.120 = log tan 7°.52,
1.470 = log ctn 1°.94,   0.962 = log sec 83°.73,
1.245 = log csc 3°.26,   8.127 = log ctn 89°.232,
15.75 =   ctn 3°.64,   100.0 =   csc 0°.573,
10.00 =   sec 84°.26,   37.71 =   tan 88°.48.

This small table may be explained by reference to the principle that *the sine and tangent of a small angle are nearly equal to the arc which is subtended by the angle in the unit-circle.* But the circumference of the unit-circle is 3.14159... Hence, the arc of 1° in that circle is $\frac{3.1416..}{180} = 0.01745..$, of which the three-place logarithm is 8.242. Then

arc φ in unit-circle = (φ in degrees) × 0.01745..,
log (arc φ in unit-circle) = log (φ in degrees) + 8.242.

This formula is exact for any angle φ, and if φ is small, it gives an approximate value of log sin φ and log tan φ, the accurate values to three places being found by substituting for 8.242 the values of S and T given in the table.

62   THE ELEMENTS OF LOGARITHMS.

(**§ 5.**) This table is directly applicable to *acute angles only*. If we have to find a function of an angle in **any other quadrant than the first**, we must subtract from the angle the greatest multiple of 90° which it contains, and then find the *same* function of the remainder if we have subtracted an *even* multiple, or the *complementary* function if we have subtracted an *odd* multiple. See formula (C). The *sign* of the result is most readily determined by observing the *quadrant* in which the given angle lies. See (D). *The sign affecting the angle* may be disregarded in the first part of the work, but must be considered in determining the quadrant. Thus, if log sin 302°.7 is required, we subtract 270° = 3 × 90°, obtaining 32°.7 as the remainder. Then, as we have subtracted an *odd* multiple,

log sin 302°.7 = log cos 32°.7 = 9.925, (neglecting signs).

But 302°.7 being in the fourth quadrant, where the sine is negative,

log sin 302°.7 = 9.925n.

In like manner we have

cos   143°.4   = — 0.803,   log tan   205°.6   = 9.680,
sin (—1055°.7) =   0.412,   log sec (—491°.8) = 0.176n,
ctn (—16°.1) = — 3.47,   log csc   120°.2   = 0.063.

In using the table *inversely* for angles in any quadrant, we should observe that any one value of a trigonometric function corresponds to *two* angles between 0° and 360°, or between —180° and +180°, or in any continuous angular space of four right angles. Thus,

if log ctn φ = 9.663n, φ = 114°.7 or = 294°.7;
if log sin φ = 9.886, φ = 50°.3 or = 129°.7;
if   cos φ = 0.810, φ = 35°.9 or = 324°.1;
if log sec φ = 0.361n, φ = 244°.2 or = 115°.8.

APPENDIX. 63

Four-Place Table of Logarithmic Trigonometric Functions.

(**§ 6.**) This table occupies five pages, the last four of which we shall consider first. These pages contain the logarithms of the sine, tangent, cotangent, and cosine, at intervals of 10′, from 5° to 85°; the characteristics, when negative, being increased by 10. The log csc and log sec are, by (A) and (§ 3), the arithmetical complements of the log sin and log cos; while the log tan and log ctn are arithmetical complements to each other. To find the logarithm of any function of any tabulated angle, we seek the *degrees*, if below 45°, in the left-hand column, and if equal to or above 45°, in the right-hand column, and take the *name* of the function on the same side of the table as the degrees, and immediately against the degrees. In the line determined by the name of the function, and in the column determined by the *minutes*, taken at the top of the table if the degrees are found at the left, and at the bottom of the table if the degrees are found at the right, will be found the second, third, and fourth decimal figures of the function. The characteristic and first decimal-figure will be found in the left-hand column of the values of the function, unless the second decimal-figure is printed in *small type*, and, in that case, they are in the right-hand column of the values of the function. E.g.,

$$\log \tan\ 8°\ 40' = 9.1831, \quad \log \sec 38°\ 00' = 0.1035,$$
$$\log \sin 18°\ 10' = 9.4939, \quad \log \csc 52°\ 00' = 0.1035,$$
$$\log \sin 18°\ 30' = 9.5015, \quad \log \sec 59°\ 50' = 0.2988,$$
$$\log \ctn 32°\ 20' = 0.1986, \quad \log \ctn 68°\ 20' = 9.5991.$$

(**§ 7.**) The functions of angles not tabulated, and lying between 5° and 85°, can be found from this table by **interpolation**, care being taken to apply the correction so as to bring the result within the proper tabular difference. To facilitate the interpolation, the proportional parts of the tabular differences (except those less than 10) occurring on the second and third pages of the table (pp. 8 and 9) are printed on those pages; while the fourth and fifth pages (pp. 10 and 11) contain the corrections for each line arranged as in the table of Logarithms of Numbers. The latter plan is inapplicable to pp. 8 and 9, because the tabular differences vary so fast that an average value cannot safely be used throughout a line.

Thus, let the functions of $7° 18'.4$ ($= 7° 20' - 1'.6$) be required. We have

	log sin	log tan	log ctn	log cos
for 7° 20'	9.1060,	9.1096,	0.8904,	9.9964,
tab diff	99,	101,	101,	2;

and the proportional parts of the tabular differences are

for 1'	9.9	10.1
for 0'.6	5.94	6.06
for 1.6	16.	16.

while $\dfrac{1.6 \times 2}{10} = 0.32$.

Then, applying the corrections so as to bring the results between the values for 7° 10' and 7° 20', we have

for 7° 18'.4

log sin $= 9.1044$, log tan $= 9.1080$, log cos $= 9.9964$,
log csc $= 0.8956$, log ctn $= 0.8920$, log sec $= 0.0036$.

Again, if the functions of $53° 47'.9$ ($= 53° 50' - 2'.1$) are required, we have

	log sin	log tan	log ctn	log cos
for 53° 50'	9.9070	0.1361,	9.8639,	9.7710,

and the lines of Proportional Parts give

	for log sin	for log tan and ctn	for log cos
for 2'	1.9	5.3	3.4
for 0'.1	0.09	0.26	0.17
for 2'.1	2.	6.	4.

APPENDIX. 65

Applying these corrections, we have
for 53° 47'.9,
log sin = 9.9068, log tan = 0.1355, log cos = 9.7714,
log csc = 0.0932, log ctn = 9.8645, log sec = 0.2286.

In like manner, we find: —

log tan 12° 41'.3 = 9.3525, log cos 37° 28'.7 = 9.8996,
log sin 18° 26'.2 = 9.5001, log ctn 51° 43'.7 = 9.8970,
log sec 69° 15'.3 = 0.4507, log csc 60° 57'.9 = 0.0583.

(§ 8.) The **first page** of this table (p. 7) contains the log sin and log tan for *every minute* from 0° to 6°, the degrees and names being given at the top, and the minutes in the left-hand column, marked ′ at the top, and the log cos and log ctn for every minute from 84° to 90°, the degrees and names being given at the bottom, and the minutes in the right-hand column marked ′ at the bottom. Only the third and fourth decimal-figures of the log tan (or log ctn) are printed, the preceding figures being the same as for the log sin (or log cos), except when the third decimal-figure of the log tan (or log ctn) is printed in small type, in which case the *second* decimal-figure is to be increased by 1. Thus: —

log sin 1° 23' = 8.3828, log cos 86° 37' = 8.7710,
log tan 1° 23' = 8.3829, log ctn 86° 37' = 8.7717,
log sin 4° 33' = 8.8994, log cos 87° 40' = 8.6097,
log tan 4° 33' = 8.9008, log ctn 87° 40' = 8.6101.

When the angle contains a fraction of a minute, interpolation may be employed; and the numbers printed in small type after the values of the functions are multipliers (*derivatives*), which may be used instead of the tabular differences through half the intervals before and after the line on which they stand, and for *both the functions* in that line. For example, to find the log sin and log tan of 1° 03'.6 (= 1° 04' — 0'.4), we have

$0.4 \times 68 = 27.2$, log sin $1°$ $03'.6 = 8.2699 - 27 = 8.2672$,
log tan $1°$ $03'.6 = 8.2700 - 27 = 8.2673$.

In like manner:—

log sin $1°$ $22'.2 = 8.3786$, log cos $87°$ $37'.8 = 8.6165$,
log tan $1°$ $22'.2 = 8.3787$, log ctn $87°$ $37'.8 = 8.6169$.

Where the printed multiplier is omitted, as in the upper part of the first column of the table, interpolation cannot properly be applied to the table, and the method which will be explained in (§ 10) must be used for angles not tabulated.

The log csc and log ctn of angles between $0°$ and $6°$ and the log sec and log tan of angles between $84°$ and $90°$ can be found by (A). Thus we have

log csc $1°$ $22'.2 = 1.6214$, log sec $87°$ $37'.8 = 1.3835$,
log ctn $1°$ $22'.2 = 1.6213$, log tan $87°$ $37'.8 = 1.3831$.

(**§ 9.**) The **right-hand division** of page 7 is a table for finding the log sec or log cos of any angle below $9°$ $51'$ or the log csc or log sin of any angle above $80°$ $09'$. The first column of this division, marked "Angles" at the top, contains those small angles, expressed to the nearest tenth of a minute, at which the last figure of the log sec and log cos expressed to four decimal places changes its value. The second column, marked "Angles" at the bottom, contains the complementary angles of the former. In the intermediate lines, and in the third column, marked "sec" at the top and "csc" at the bottom, are the third and fourth decimal figures of the log sec of the angles which lie between those named in the first column, and of the log csc of the angles between those named in the second column; the preceding figures, which are always 0.00, being given at the top and bottom of the column. Thus, 0.0006 is the log sec (to four places) of any angle between $2°$ $53'.0$ and $3°$ $08'.0$ and the log csc of any angle between $86°$ $52'.0$ and $87°$ $07'.0$.

APPENDIX. 67

The arithmetical complement of the tabulated logarithm is the log cos or log sin of the given angle. Thus, we have

log sec 1° 22′.2 = 0.0001, log csc 87° 37′.8 = 0.0004,
log cos 1° 22′.2 = 9.9999, log sin 87° 37′.8 = 9.9996.

This little table leads us to observe the *slow rate of variation* of the cos and sec when their angle is near 0°, and of the sin and csc when their angle is near 90°. Hence a small angle cannot be very accurately found from its cos or sec, or an angle near 90° from its sin or csc; for the function, or its logarithm, expressed to a given number of places, may correspond to *any angle included within a considerable range*. See also (§ 17).

(§ 10.) The log sin, log tan, log csc, and log ctn of small angles and the log cos, log ctn, log sec, and log tan of angles near 90° can also be found by the small tables at the bottom of the table of **Logarithms of Numbers**, which correspond to that explained in (§ 4). We must find the logarithm of the given angle (or of its complement in the case of an angle near 90°) in *minutes*, and for this purpose we may generally use the extreme left-hand column of the table of logarithms, headed "Angles," without reducing the angle to minutes. Thus:—

log sin 4° 23′.6 = 2.4209 + 6.4633 = 8.8842,
log tan 4° 23′.6 = 2.4209 + 6.4646 = 8.8855,
log sin 1° 03′.6 = 1.8035 + 6.4637 = 8.2672,
log tan 1° 03′.6 = 1.8035 + 6.4638 = 8.2673,
log cos 87° 37′.8 = log sin 2° 22′.2
        = 2.1529 + 6.4636 = 8.6165,
log ctn 87° 37′.8 = 2.1529 + 6.4640 = 8.6169,
log ctn 89° 59′.90127 = log tan 0° 00′.09873
        = 8.9944 + 6.4637 = 5.4581.

(**§ 11.**) The functions of **angles in all quadrants** may be found by the method which has already been explained in (§ 5). The table at the top of page 10, the arrangement of which will be readily understood, may be used in this connexion. E.g.: —

$$\log \sin\ 97°\ 18'.4 = 9.9964,$$
$$\log \operatorname{ctn}\ 413°\ 47'.9 = 9.8645,$$
$$\log \tan\ 192°\ 41'.3 = 9.3525n,$$
$$\log \cos\ (-108°\ 26'.2) = 9.5001n,$$
$$\log \csc\ 339°\ 15'.3 = 0.4507n,$$
$$\log \cos\ (-37°\ 28'.7) = 9.8996,$$
$$\log \sec\ 590°\ 27'.0 = 0.1960n,$$
$$\log \sin\ 178°\ 56'.4 = 8.2672.$$

(**§ 12.**) In astronomy, angles are sometimes expressed in **time**, instead of *arc*, the circle being divided into 24 hours.

The angles in our table are accordingly expressed in this system, as well as in degrees and minutes. This is the case with all the angles in the principal table of p. 7, and with the exact *degrees* on the other pages of the table, little tables for converting minutes into time and time into minutes being given on each of those pages, in the corners of the main table. Thus, we have

$$\log \sin\ 0^h\ 10^m\ 08^s = 8.6454,\ \log \operatorname{ctn}\ 2^h\ 31^m\ 15^s = 0.1101,$$
$$\log \csc\ 5^h\ 33^m\ 20^s = 0.0029,\ \log \sec\ 4^h\ 09^m\ 53^s = 0.3352.$$

(**§ 13.**) In navigation and surveying, horizontal angles are often expressed in **points of the compass**, of which *eight* constitute the quadrant, and *one* is equal to 11° 15'. At the top of page 11 will be found a table of logarithmic trigonometric functions for every quarter-point. The points at the top are to be used with the names on the left, and the points at the bottom with the names on the right. Thus, we have

log sin 1¼ pt = 9.3856,   log ctn 5½ pt = 9.7280,
log sec 7   pt = 0.7098, log cos 10½ pt = 9.6734.

Interpolation should not be applied to the compass-table.

Inverse Trigonometric Functions.

(**§ 14.**) The angle which corresponds to a given value of any logarithmic trigonometric function may be found by the inverse use of the table explained above, in (§§ 6-13). But a more convenient way of arriving at the angle is furnished by the table of *Inverse Trigonometric Functions*. In the headings of this table, A denotes *any trigonometric function*, log A its *logarithm*, and $\sin^{-1} A$, $\cos^{-1} A$, &c., *the angle of which A is the sine, cosine*, &c., as the case may be. This is in accordance with custom and with the principle of notation explained in Logarithms, § **34**. The symbol $\sin^{-1}$ may be read *inverse sine*, or *antisine*, or *the angle* (or *arc*) *of which the sine is*. It is sometimes denoted by "arcsin." Thus we have

$$\log^{-1} = \text{antilog}, \quad \sin^{-1} = \text{arcsin}.$$

The inverse of "log sin" may be written in either of the following ways: —

$$(\log \sin)^{-1} = \sin^{-1} \log^{-1} = \text{arcsin antilog}.$$

The *argument* of this table is the logarithmic trigonometric function (the characteristic being increased by 10, when negative), and is denoted by log A. In the *first three divisions* of the table, occupying page 12 and the first half of page 13, the argument is given, at intervals of 0.01, from 8.5000 (— 10) to 0.0000 in the left-hand column of the table, and from 0.0000 to 1.5000 in the right-hand column of the table. The names at the top are to be taken with the left-hand column, and the names at the bottom with the right-hand column. Thus, *under* the name $\sin^{-1} A$, $\cos^{-1} A$, $\tan^{-1} A$, or $\ctn^{-1} A$, and in the same line with a value of log A, found at the *left*, is the angle of which that value of log A is the log sin, log cos, log tan, or log ctn; and *over* the name $\tan^{-1} A$, $\ctn^{-1} A$, $\sec^{-1} A$, or $\csc^{-1} A$, and in the same line with log A at the *right*, is the angle of which log A is the log tan, log ctn, log sec, or log csc. E.g.: —

$$(\log \sin)^{-1}\ 8.8200 = 3° \ 47'.3,$$
$$(\log \tan)^{-1}\ 9.7400 = 28° \ 47',$$
$$(\log \csc)^{-1}\ 0.7800 = 9° \ 33',$$
$$(\log \cos)^{-1}\ 9.0700 = 83° \ 15',$$
$$(\log \ctn)^{-1}\ 0.1000 = 38° \ 28',$$
$$(\log \sec)^{-1}\ 1.4200 = 87° \ 49'.3.$$

The angle corresponding to a non-tabulated value of log A may be found by direct interpolation; and the number in small type on the right or left of any tabulated angle is a multiplier (*derivative*) which may be used, instead of the tabular difference, in this interpolation, through half the interval before and after the angle against which it stands, being so pointed off as to express the number of minutes by which the angle is varied in that part of the table, by a change of *one unit in the third decimal-place* of log A. The general table of Proportional Parts (p. 2) may be used in finding the correction.

For instance, suppose we have to find the angle of which the log sin is $8.9023 (-10)$.

We have, if log $A = 8.9000$, $\sin^{-1} A = 4° \ 33'.4$;
by table of Proportional Parts, $0'.63 \times 2.3 = \ 1'.4$;
whence, if log $A = 8.9023$, $\sin^{-1} A = 4° \ 34'.8$;
adding so as to approach the value for 8.9100.

Next, to find $(\log \ctn)^{-1}\ 9.7984\ (-10)$: —

We have, if log $A = 9.8000$
 ($= 9.7984 + 0.0016$),   ctn^{-1} $A = 57°\ 45'$;
by table of Proportional Parts, $3'.6 \times 1.6 = \quad 6'$;
whence, if log $A = 9.7984$,   ctn^{-1} $A = 57°\ 51'$;
again *adding*, so as to approach the value for 9.7900.

Again, to find (log sec)$^{-1}$ 0.5157 :—
We have, if log $A = 0.5200$
 ($= 0.5157 + 0.0043$),   sec^{-1} $A = 72°\ 25'$;
by table of Proportional Parts, $2'.5 \times 4.3 = \quad 11'$;
whence, if log $A = 0.5157$,   sec^{-1} $A = 72°\ 14'$;
subtracting so as to approach the value for 0.5100.

In like manner, let the student find the following results:—

$$(\log \tan)^{-1}\ 0.6931 = 78°\ 33',$$
$$(\log \csc)^{-1}\ 1.3574 = 2°\ 31'.0,$$
$$(\log \sin)^{-1}\ 9.0590 = 6°\ 35',$$
$$(\log \cos)^{-1}\ 9.6062 = 66°\ 11',$$
$$(\log \tan)^{-1}\ 8.9507 = 5°\ 06'.1,$$
$$(\log \ctn)^{-1}\ 0.5555 = 15°\ 33'.$$

The angle is, in every case, to be found with the same degree of accuracy as that of the tabulated angles between which it is interpolated; that is, to the nearest tenth of a minute if found from the first division of the table, and otherwise to the nearest minute. The reason of the difference is that the angle varies less rapidly at the beginning of the table than at the end for a given change in log A, and hence is more accurately determined by a value of log A given to four places. Towards the end of the table, it is sometimes not even determined to the nearest minute, as we shall presently explain more particularly. See (§ 17).

(**§ 15.**) The student should remark that the angles in the columns of sin^{-1} A and cos^{-1} A are *complements* of each other; also in those of $\tan^{-1} A$ and $\ctn^{-1} A$; and again in those of $\sec^{-1} A$ and $\csc^{-1} A$. This is in accordance with (B).

Again, the values of the argument on opposite sides of the page are *arithmetical complements*, and therefore correspond to *reciprocal* values of A; while the angles bear to these values of A reciprocal relations, as the upper and lower names of the same column ($\sin^{-1} A$ and $\csc^{-1} A$; $\cos^{-1} A$ and $\sec^{-1} A$; &c.) indicate. See (A).

(**§ 16.**) The multipliers for the first and second columns are omitted in the lower half of the third division of the table; because in that part of the table they vary too rapidly to admit of accurate interpolation through so wide an interval as 0.01. Hence, the **last three divisions** of the table are given, containing the argument *at smaller intervals*, from 9.7500 to 0.0000, the multipliers being still so expressed as to measure the variation in minutes for a change of 0.001 in the argument. Thus, we find:—

If $\log \sin \varphi = 9.8236$, $\varphi = 41° 56' - 1.4 \times 7'.1 = 41° 46'$;
if $\log \sin \varphi = 9.8812$, $\varphi = 49° 39' - 0.8 \times 9'.3 = 49° 32'$;
if $\log \sin \varphi = 9.9173$, $\varphi = 55° 42' + 0.3 \times 12' = 55° 46'$.

The values of $\cos^{-1} A$ are the complements of those of $\sin^{-1} A$; and the arithmetical complements of the tabulated values of $\log A$ are the values of the log csc for the angles in the column $\sin^{-1} A$, and of the log sec for the complements of those angles. Thus, we have:—

If $\log \cos \varphi = 9.9267$, $\sin^{-1} A = 57° 38'$, $\varphi = 32° 22$;
if $\log \csc \varphi = 0.0265$, $\log \sin \varphi = 9.9735$, $\varphi = 70° 11'$;
if $\log \sec \varphi = 0.1089$, $\log \cos \varphi = 9.8911$, $\varphi = 38° 54'$;
  if $\log \cos \varphi = 9.8183$, $\varphi = 48° 51'$;
  if $\log \sec \varphi = 0.1252$, $\varphi = 41° 27'$;
  if $\log \csc \varphi = 0.1879$, $\varphi = 40° 27'$;
  if $\log \sec \varphi = 0.1999$, $\varphi = 50° 52'$.

(§ **17.**) When a change of 0.0001 in any logarithmic trigonometric function produces a change of more than 1' in the corresponding angle, *the four-place logarithm does not determine the logarithm to minutes*, since the uncertainty of ±0.00005 in the logarithm will leave an uncertainty of ±0'.5 in the angle. This is never the case with the log tan or log ctn; but an angle can always be found to minutes from either of these functions and by means of the first three divisions of the table. But with the other functions this uncertainty may occur; and the point at which it begins (at log $A = 9.8940$ or $= 0.1060$) is indicated by a note in the table. The angles are, however, still tabulated to minutes, and the given values may be regarded as the *probable* values for the assumed values of the functions. Thus, if log sin $\varphi = 9.9900$, of which the true value may lie anywhere between 9.98995 and 9.99005, φ may have any value from 77° 43' to 77° 47'. But if 9.9900 expresses the value of the logarithm *exactly*, $\varphi = 77°$ 45', which is therefore adopted as the probable value.

At the bottom of the last column of the table, interpolation becomes inaccurate. But the *uncertainty* just spoken of is here so great that the angle cannot be determined with nicety from the given function; and the inaccuracy of interpolation is, therefore, of little consequence.

It is to be observed that, with four-place logarithms, the angle can be determined to minutes from its *log tan* or *log ctn* in *all parts of the quadrant;* from its *log sin* or *log csc* in the *first half* of the quadrant; and from its *log cos* or *log sec* in the *last half*. This observation will often direct the computer in the choice of his method, where several are open to him.

(§ **18.**) This table is only applicable to values of the logarithm between 8.5000 (— 10) and 1.5000. If the logarithm lies outside of these limits, the angle may be found by the table of **Logarithms of Numbers**, by the formula printed between the two divisions of page 12, which is obtained by reversing those at the bottom of pp. 4 and 5. For those formulas give

$$\log (\varphi \text{ in minutes}) = \log \sin \varphi - S = \log \tan \varphi - T.$$

Hence, if $S = T = 6.4637$, we have

$$\log (\varphi \text{ in minutes}) = \log A + 3.5363 - 10,$$

whether A denotes sin φ or tan φ. S has always the above value, when $\log A < 8.5000$, but T may reach the value 6.4639, and thus give a (generally unimportant) correction of our formula.

If the given logarithm is the log cos or log ctn of the required angle, that angle will be the complement of φ determined as above. If $\log A > 1.5000$, we must take its arithmetical complement, which will be the logarithm of the reciprocal function, and proceed as above.

Thus:—

If $\log \sin \varphi = 7.5192,\quad \log \varphi = 1.0555,\ \varphi = 11'.36$;
if $\log \cos \varphi = 8.0079,\quad \log \text{co } \varphi = 1.5442,\ \text{co } \varphi = 35'.01,$
$\quad \varphi = 89°\ 24'.99$;
if $\log \tan \varphi = 6.8197,\quad \log \varphi = 0.3560,\ \varphi = 2'.270$;
if $\log \text{ctn } \varphi = 1.9981,\ \log \tan \varphi = 8.0019,\ \varphi = 34'.53$;
if $\log \sec \varphi = 1.5019,\ \log \cos \varphi = 8.4981,\ \varphi = 88°\ 11'.7$;
if $\log \csc \varphi = 4.1254,\ \log \sin \varphi = 5.8746,\ \varphi = 0'.2576$.

(§ **19.**) Acute angles only are directly given by this table. When **angles in any quadrant** are admissible, the *signs* of the given trigonometric functions must be noted, and it must be remembered that to every value of any function *two angles* correspond, in any four consecutive right angles; for example, between 0° and 360°, or be-

APPENDIX. 75

tween $-180°$ and $+180°$. The values of the angles may be found from the table by the aid of (C). Thus:—

$(\log \sin)^{-1}$ $8.9023n = 184° 34'.8$ or $= 355° 25'.2$;
$(\log \operatorname{ctn})^{-1}$ $9.7984 = 57° 51$ or $= 237° 51'$;
$(\log \sec)^{-1}$ $0.5157n = 107° 46'$ or $= 252° 14'$;
$(\log \tan)^{-1}$ $0.6931n = 101° 27'$ or $= 281° 27'$;
$(\log \cos)^{-1}$ $9.6062 = 66° 11'$ or $= -66° 11'$;
$(\log \sin)^{-1}$ $9.0590 = 6° 35'$ or $= 173° 25'$.

In many questions, the required angle can only be *acute* or *obtuse*. It is then fully determined by the *sign* of the given function, unless that function is a *sine* or *cosecant;* and, in that case, two values of the angle are admissible if the function is positive, none if the function is negative. Thus, in such a question:—

$(\log \operatorname{ctn})^{-1}$ $0.5555n = 164° 27'$;
$(\log \sin)^{-1}$ $9.8236 = 41° 46'$ or $= 138° 14'$;
$(\log \cos)^{-1}$ $9.9267 = 32° 22'$;
$(\log \sin)^{-1}$ $9.8812n$ is an inadmissible angle.

(§ **20.**) This table can also be used **inversely** to find a logarithmic trigonometric function of a given angle; and if we were restricted to *one* trigonometric table, it would probably be found more convenient to use this table both directly and inversely than that which precedes it.

Let the student find from this table:—

log tan 57° 46' $= 0.2003$, log sec 50° 27' $= 0.1961$,
log cos 63° 56' $= 9.6429$, log sin 4° 23'.6 $= 8.8843$,
log ctn 4° 23'.6 $= 1.1144$, log ctn 87° 37'.8 $= 8.6170$.

(§ **21.**) If the **natural value** to four figures of any trigonometric function of a given angle, or the angle which corresponds to such a value, is required, we must use the table of Logarithms of Numbers, in connexion with one of the four-place trigonometric tables. Thus: —

$\tan\ 57° 46' = 1.586, \quad \sin\ 4° 23'.6 = 0.0766,$
$\sec^{-1} 26.30 = 87° 49'.3, \quad \ctn^{-1} 0.8217 = 50° 36'.$

Examples in Trigonometry for the Four-Place Tables.

Seaver's Formulas of Trigonometry (Boston, John Allyn) will be found a convenient book of reference in these examples.

(§ **22**.) *Plane Right Triangles.*

Ex. 1. Given: $h = 0.4958$, $A = 54° 44'$.

$h = 0.4958$	log	9.6953		9.6953
$A = 54° 44'$	log sin	9.9120	log cos	9.7615
	log a	9.6073	log b	9.4568
$B = 90° - A = 35° 16'$		$a = 0.4048$		$b = 0.2863$

Ex. 2. Given: $h = 54.57$, $a = 23.48$.

$h = 54.57$			colog	8.2630
$a = 23.48$			log	1.3707
$h + a = 78.05$	log	1.8924	log sin A log cos B	9.6337
$h - a = 31.09$	log	1.4927	$A = 25° 29'$	
	2)3.3851		$B = 64° 31'$	
	log b	1.6926	$b = 49.28$	

Ex. 3. Given: $a = 0.04437$, $b = 0.02216$.

$a = 0.04437$	log	8.6471		8.6471
$b = 0.02216$	colog	1.6544		
$A = 63° 28'$	log tan log ctn	0.3015	log csc log sec	0.0483
$B = 26° 32'$				
$h = 0.04959$			log	8.6954

We may also find h by the Gaussian table, as in Logarithms, § **66**.

APPENDIX. 77

Ex. 4. Given: $h = 0.3736, B = 12° 30'$.
To be computed: $A = 77° 30', a = 0.3648, b = 0.08086$.

Ex. 5. Given: $b = 14.548, B = 54° 24'$.
To be computed: $A = 35° 36', h = 17.888, a = 10.415$.

Ex. 6. Given: $b = 11.111, A = 11° 11'$.
To be computed: $B = 78° 49', h = 11.324, a = 2.196$.

Ex. 7. Given: $h = 0.06723, b = 0.05489$.
To be computed: $a = 0.03882, A = 35° 16, B = 54° 44'$.

Ex. 8. Given: $a = 8.148, b = 10.864$.
To be computed: $h = 13.58, A = 36° 53', B = 53° 07'$.

(§ **23.**) *Special Cases of Plane Right Triangles.*
Seaver's Formulas, 130.

Ex. 1. Given: $h = 4602.8360, b = 4602.2106$.

$h - b =$ 0.6254   log   9.7962
$2h =$ 9205.6720   colog 6.0359
                          ─────────────
                          2)5.8321
$\tfrac{1}{2}A$ log sin 7.9160
                                  3.5363
$\tfrac{1}{2}A = 0° 28'.33$ log 1.4523
$A = 0° 56'.66$ $B = 89° 03'.34$

Ex. 2. Given: $a = 3792.8714, b = 3791.8692$.

$a = 3792.8714$ colog 6.4211
$b = 3791.8692$ colog 6.4212
$a - b =$ 1.0022   log 0.0009
$a + b = 7584.7406$ log 3.8800
        2.   colog 9.6990
                        ─────────────
$A - B$ log tan 6.4222
                                3.5363
                        ─────────────
$A - B =$ 0° 00'.9088   log 9.9585
$A + B = 90° 00'.0000$
  $A = 45° 00'.4544$ $B = 44° 59'.5456$.

Ex. 3. Given: $h = 210.54219$, $a = 210.48823$.

$$
\begin{array}{ll}
h - a = 0.05396 & \log 8.7321 \\
2h = 421.08438 & \operatorname{colog} 7.3756 \\
& \overline{2)6.1077} \\
45° - \tfrac{1}{2}A & \log \sin 8.0538 \\
& 3.5363 \\
45° - \tfrac{1}{2}A = 0° 38'.92 & \log 1.5901 \\
\tfrac{1}{2}A = 44° 21'.08 & \\
A = 88° 42'.16 & B = 1° 17'.84
\end{array}
$$

Ex. 4. Given: $h = 107.9823$, $B = 2° \, 08'.64$.

To be computed: $a = 107.8867$, $b = 4.040$, $A = 87° \, 51'.36$.

Ex. 5. Given: $a = 920139$, $b = 925897$.

To be computed: $A = 44° \, 49'.27$, $B = 45° \, 10'.73$.

Ex. 6. Given: $h = 2.096889$, $A = 86° \, 25'.38$.

To be computed: $a = 2.092802$, $b = 0.1308$, $B = 3° \, 34'.62$.

(§ 24.) *Plane Oblique Triangles.*

Ex. 1. Given: $a = 0.3578$, $B = 32° 41'$, $C = 47° \, 54'$.

$A = 180° - (B + C) = 99° \, 25'$.

$$
\begin{array}{llll|lll}
a = 0.3578 & \log & 9.5537 & & & & 9.5537 \\
B = 32° \, 41' & \log \sin & 9.7324 & C = 47° \, 54' & \log \sin & 9.8704 \\
A = 99° \, 25' & \log \csc & 0.0059 & & & & 0.0059 \\
b = 0.1959 & \log & \overline{9.2920} & c = 0.2691 & \log & & \overline{9.4300}
\end{array}
$$

Ex. 2. Given: $c = 325.06$, $A = 154° \, 22'$, $C = 8° \, 03'$.

To be computed: $B = 17° \, 35'$, $a = 1004.3$, $b = 701.2$.

Ex. 3.* Given: $a = 4236$, $b = 5124$, $B = 124° \, 50'$.

---

* Each of the examples 3–9 should be illustrated by a figure.

APPENDIX. 79

$a = 4236$ log 3.6270
$b = 5124$ colog 6.2904   log 3.7096   3.7096
$B = 124°\ 50'$ log sin 9.9142 log csc 0.0858   0.0858
$A_1 = 42°\ 44'$ log sin 9.8316
$A_2 = 137°\ 16'$
$C_1 = 12°\ 26'$ log sin 9.3330
$C_2 = -82°\ 06'$ log sin $9.9959n$
                                 log 3.1284   log $3.7913n$
                                 $c_1 = 1344$ $c_2 = -6184$

Ex. 4. Given: $a = 4236$, $b = 5124$, $A = 124°\ 50'$.

Compute: $B_1 = 83°\ 04'$, $C_1 = -27°\ 54'$, $c_1 = -2416$.
$B_2 = 96°\ 56'$, $C_2 = -41°\ 46'$, $c_2 = -3438$.

Ex. 5. Given: $a = 49.00$, $c = 67.98$, $C = 32°\ 18'$.
Compute: $A_1 = 22°\ 39'$, $B_1 = 125°\ 03'$, $b_1 = 104.17$;
$A_2 = 157°\ 21'$, $B_2 = -9°\ 39'$, $b_2 = -21.32$.

Ex. 6. Given: $a = 49.00$, $c = 49.00$, $C = 32°\ 18'$.
Compute: $A_1 = 32°\ 18'$, $B_1 = 115°\ 24'$, $b_1 = 82.84$;
$A_2 = 147°\ 42'$, $B_2 = 0°\ 00'$, $b_2 = 0$.

Ex. 7. Given: $a = 49.00$, $c = 31.24$, $C = 32°\ 18'$.
Compute: $A_1 = 56°\ 57'$, $B_1 = 90°\ 45'$, $b_1 = 58.46$;
$A_2 = 123°\ 03'$, $B_2 = 24°\ 39'$, $b_2 = 24.38$.

Ex. 8. Given: $a = 49.00$, $c = 26.18$, $C = 32°\ 18'$.
To be computed: $A_1 = A_2 = 90°\ 00'$, $B_1 = B_2 = 57°\ 42'$,
$b_1 = b_2 = 41.42$.

Ex. 9. Given: $a = 49.00$, $c = 12.50$, $C = 32°\ 18'$.

We find log sin $A = 0.3211$. ∴ sin $A > 1$, which is impossible, and there is no triangle which satisfies the conditions.

Ex. 10. Given: $a = 6.239$, $b = 2.348$, $C = 110°\ 32'$.

$$a+b = 8.587 \qquad \text{colog } 9.0662$$
$$a-b = 3.891 \qquad \text{log } 0.5900$$
$$90° - \tfrac{1}{2}C = \tfrac{1}{2}(A+B) = 34° \; 44' \quad \text{log tan } 9.8409$$
$$\tfrac{1}{2}(A-B) = 17° \; 26' \quad \text{log tan } 9.4971$$
$$A = 52° \; 10'$$
$$B = 17° \; 18' \quad \text{log csc } 0.5267$$
$$C = 110° \; 32' \quad \text{log sin } 9.9715$$
$$b = 2.348 \qquad \text{log } 0.3707$$
$$c = 7.395 \qquad \text{log } 0.8689$$

The side c can also be found in the following ways:—

$$(a+b) \text{ log } \quad 0.9338 \qquad (a-b) \text{ log } \quad 0.5900$$
$$\tfrac{1}{2}(A+B) \text{ log cos } 9.9147 \qquad\qquad \text{log sin } 9.7557$$
$$\tfrac{1}{2}(A-B) \text{ log sec } 0.0204 \qquad\qquad \text{log csc } 0.5235$$
$$c = 7.395 \text{ log } \quad 0.8689 \quad c = 7.400 \text{ log } \quad 0.8692$$

$\tfrac{1}{2}(A-B)$ is so small that the slight error in its computed value gives rise to a perceptible error in its log csc, and therefore in c as computed by the last formula.

Ex. 11. Given: $a = 0.01511$, $c = 0.03100$, $B = 169°\;45'$.

To be computed: $A = 3°\;21'.3$, $C = 6°\;53'.7$, $b = 0.2541$.

Ex. 12. Given: $a = 0.13561$, $b = 0.12348$, $c = 0.14091$.

$$s = 0.20000 \qquad \text{colog } 0.6990$$
$$s - a = 0.06439 \qquad \text{log } 8.8088 \quad \text{co } 1.1912$$
$$s - b = 0.07652 \qquad \text{log } 8.8838 \quad \text{co } 1.1162$$
$$s - c = 0.05909 \qquad \text{log } 8.7715 \quad \text{co } 1.2285$$
$$2)17.1631$$
$$\text{log } r \; 8.5816 \qquad 8.5816$$

$$A = 61°\;18' \quad \tfrac{1}{2}A = 30°\;39' \quad \text{log tan } 9.7728$$
$$B = 53°\;00' \quad \tfrac{1}{2}B = 26°\;30' \quad \text{log tan } 9.6978$$
$$C = 65°\;42' \quad \tfrac{1}{2}C = 32°\;51' \quad \text{log tan } 9.8101$$
$$2S = 180°\;00'$$

Ex. 13. Given: $a = 17.856$, $b = 13.349$, $c = 11.111$.
To be computed: $A = 93° 20'$, $B = 48° 16'$, $C = 38° 24'$.

Ex. 14. Given: $a = 32.571$, $A = 29° 47'.61$, $B = 33° 10'.37$.
Compute by Seaver, **131**, *Third Method:* $b = 35.868$.

Ex. 15. Given: $C = 121° 42'$, log $a = 1.8968$, log $b = 2.0014$.
Compute by Seaver, **133**, *Second Method:* $A = 25° 20'$, $B = 32° 58'$.

Ex. 16. Given: $a = 0.062387$, $b = 0.023475$, $C = 110° 32'$.
Compute by Seaver, **133**, *Third Method:* $c = 0.07395$.

(§ **25.**) *Heights and Distances.*

Ex. 1. At the distance of 277.3 feet from a tower, which stands on a horizontal plane, the angle of elevation of the tower is observed to be $37° 28'$. Find its height.
Ans. 217.5 feet.

Ex. 2. From the top of a tower 367.6 feet high, an object is observed in the horizontal plane on which the tower stands, with an angle of depression of $49° 43'$. Find the distance of the object from the foot of the tower. *Ans.* 311.4 feet.

Ex. 3. Two observers, stationed on opposite sides of a cloud, observe the angles of elevation to be $51° 23'$ and $30° 18'$, their distance apart being 1000 feet. Find the height of the cloud and its distances from the two observers. *Ans.* 2712 feet; 3472 feet; 5401 feet.

Ex. 4. The angle of elevation of the top of a tower, which stands on a horizontal plane, is observed at one station to be $68° 19'$, and at another station, 546 feet farther from the tower, to be $32° 34'$. Find the height of the tower, and its distances from the two points of observation. *Ans.* 467.6 feet; 185.9 feet; 731.9 feet.

Ex. 5. An observer on shipboard sees a cape bearing N.N.E.; and after sailing 30 miles N.W. by N., he sees the same cape bearing E. by S. Find the distances of the cape from the two points of observation. *Ans.* 21.65 miles; 25.43 miles. This example is most easily solved by finding the angles in points (namely, 5 pts, 4 pts, and 7 pts), and then using the table at the top of p. 11 of the Tables.

Ex. 6. Coasting along shore, I saw a cape of land bearing N.N.E.; and after sailing W.N.W. 20 miles, I saw it bearing N.E. by E. Find the distances of the cape from the ship at both stations. *Ans.* 29.93 miles; 36.00 miles.

Ex. 7. Being at sea, we saw two headlands, of which one bore S.W. by W. and the other W. by N. The chart showed that the first headland bore S.E. from the second, and was distant from it 23.25 miles. Find our distances from both headlands. *Ans.* 18.26 miles; 32.25 miles.

Ex. 8. Two ships sail from the same port, the one S.W. 30 miles, and the other S.E. by S. 40 miles. Find the bearing and distance of the second ship from the first. *Ans.* S. 74° 30′ W.; 45.08 miles.

Ex. 9. An observer from a ship saw two headlands; the first bearing N.E. by E., and the second N.W. After he had sailed N.N.W. 10.25 miles, the first headland bore E. by N., and the second W.N.W. Find the bearing and distance of the first headland from the second. *Ans.* N. 88° 02′ E., or nearly due east; 35.25 miles.

Ex 10. An observer saw two headlands; the first bearing S.E., the second E.S.E. After sailing E. by N. 10 miles, he saw the first bearing S. by E., and the second

S.E. by S. Find the bearing and distance of the first headland from the second. *Ans.* S.S.W. 6.89 miles.

Ex. 11. At one station, the bearing of a cloud is N.N.W., and its angle of elevation 50° 35′. At a second station, bearing from the first N. by E. and distant 1 mile, the bearing of the cloud is W. by N. Find the height of the cloud and its distance from each station.
Ans. 7727 feet; 10002 feet; 8838 feet.

Ex. 12. In the midst of a level plain, which is crossed by a straight road, stands a tower, 250 feet high. An observer at the top of the tower sees an object which moves on the road. At first, it bears N.N.W., and its angle of depression is 16° 08′; five minutes later, it bears E. by S., and its angle of depression is 32° 18′. Find the direction of the road, its distance from the tower, and the rate at which the object is moving.
Ans. S.E. ½ S.; 250.9 feet; 2.575 miles per hour.

(§ **26.**) *Areas of Triangles.*

Ex. 1. Given: $a = 12.34$ chains, $b = 17.97$ chains, $C = 135° 04$.
To be computed: Area $= 7.832$ acres $= 7$A 3R 13r.

Ex. 2. Given: $a = 17.95$ chains, $B = 100°$, $C = 70°$.
To be computed: Area $= 85.90$ acres $= 85$A 3R 24r.

Ex. 3. Given: $a = 45.56$ chains, $b = 52.98$ chains, $c = 61.22$ chains.
To be computed: Area $= 117.3$ acres $= 117$A 1.2R.

Ex. 4. Given: $a = 32.56$ chains, $b = 57.84$ chains, $c = 44.44$ chains.
To be computed: Area $= 71.93$ acres $= 71$A 3R 29r.

www.ingramcontent.com/pod-product-compliance
Lightning Source LLC
Chambersburg PA
CBHW020301090426
42735CB00009B/1179